LEARNING TO BELIEVE

*A Meditation on the
Christian Creed*

CARROLL E. SIMCOX

FORTRESS PRESS   PHILADELPHIA

COPYRIGHT © 1981 BY FORTRESS PRESS

Library of Congress Cataloging in Publication Data
Simcox, Carroll Eugene, 1912–
    Learning to believe.

    1. Meditations.   I. Title.
BV4832.2.S5258   230   80-2372
ISBN 0-8006-1497-6

8560J80   Printed in the United States of America   1-1497

This book is lovingly dedicated to all my spiritual pastors and masters, now in the Father's House, who have helped, and still help, me learn to believe. They, being dead, yet speak.

Acknowledgments

Acknowledgments are gratefully made to the following publishers and holders of copyright for their permissions to quote material used in the text of this book.

To Harper & Row, Publishers, Inc., for passages from John Donne, *The Showing Forth of Christ*, ed. by Edmund Fuller; Pierre Teilhard de Chardin, *The Phenomenon of Man*; Pierre Teilhard de Chardin, *Hymn of the Universe*; and Pierre Teilhard de Chardin, *The Divine Milieu.*

To Morehouse-Barlow Co., Inc., for passages from Carroll E. Simcox, *Living the Lord's Prayer*, and Sergius Bulgakov, *The Orthodox Church.*

To A. P. Watt, Ltd., for a quotation from Gilbert Keith Chesterton, *Heretics.*

To St. Martin's Press, Inc., for two passages from A. E. Taylor, *The Faith of a Moralist.*

To Charles Scribner's Sons, for a quotation from J. Jeremias, *The Parables of Jesus*, 6th ed., trans. by S. H. Hooke.

To Macmillan Publishing Co., Inc., for material from Alfred North Whitehead, *Religion in the Making* (copyright 1926 by Macmillan Publishing Co., Inc., renewed 1954 by Evelyn Whitehead); Dietrich Bonhoeffer, *Letters and Papers from Prison* (copyright 1953, 1967, 1971 by SCM Press Ltd.); Harvey Cox, *The Secular City*, rev. ed., (copyright Harvey Cox 1965, 1966); and C. S. Lewis, *Mere Christianity* (copyright 1943, 1945, 1952 by Macmillan Publishing Co., Inc.).

To Simon & Schuster, a Division of Gulf & Western Corporation, for a quotation from Bertrand Russell, *A History of Western Philosophy* (copyright 1945, 1972 by Bertrand Russell).

To Donnan and Garth Jeffers, for a quotation from Robinson Jeffers's poem, "The Coast-Range Christ."

Contents

1

Creedal Meditation

Reverie is the Sunday of thought; and who knows
which is the more important and fruitful for man,
the laborious tension of the week, or the life-
giving repose of the Sabbath?

Henri Frédéric Amiel, *Journal*, April 29, 1852

The great Victorians Thomas Carlyle and Bishop Samuel
Wilberforce were talking about death when Carlyle asked,
"Bishop, have you a creed?" "Yes," Wilberforce replied, "I
have a creed, and the older I grow the firmer it becomes;
there is only one thing that staggers me." "What is that?"
asked Carlyle. "It is the slow progress that creed makes in the
world," replied the bishop. Carlyle was silent for a moment,
then replied gravely, "Ah, but if you have a creed you can
afford to wait."

It was a ponderable remark, like everything Carlyle said.
But is it true of any and every creed? Your creed is that which
you ultimately believe about ultimate reality. It may be fat-
uous nonsense or a vicious falsehood: for example, the Nazi
creed of the divine mission of the *Herrenvolk* to rule the
world. With a false creed people may think that they can
"afford to wait" and do immeasurable harm to themselves
and others while waiting. If Carlyle had said, "Ah, Bishop,
with *your* creed you can afford to wait," he would have made
full sense.

Wilberforce's creed is the Christian creed. Armed with
that, the believer can afford to wait for God to finish in glory
all that he is now creating in his unfinished world, and be sure
that in that divine triumph all of God's people who now put

their trust in him will themselves be glorified and rejoice in the eternal victory.

But the Christian creed should do more for believers than to enable them to wait for the New Heaven and the New Earth. It should enable them, while they wait—while they strive and pray and stumble forward and fall and suffer defeats—to know joy in the midst of pain, peace in strife, and assurance of victory when they seem hopelessly beaten.

Over the past forty-odd years it has done so for me. There was a moment in my early twenties when, in John Wesley's phrase, I felt my heart strangely warmed. Wesley's moment was when he listened to a preacher reading Luther's preface to his commentary on Romans. My moment was when I joined a congregation in reciting the Nicene Creed, which was then new to me. "Then felt I like some watcher of the skies when a new planet swims into his ken."

At the same time in my life I became acquainted with the Anglican *Book of Common Prayer*. In studying it, I came to the Catechism, in which the catechumens are asked what they chiefly learn from the Creed, and they reply:

"First, I learn to believe in God the Father, who hath made me, and all the world.

"Secondly, in God the Son, who hath redeemed me, and all mankind.

"Thirdly, in God the Holy Ghost, who sanctifieth me, and all the people of God."

Being young at the time, I had no sense of the meaning of "learning to believe." Now, in my late sixties, I do. Christians must spend their whole mortal lives learning to believe; and I shall not be greatly surprised to learn, in due course, that this learning will continue everlastingly as we forever grow in the knowledge and love of God. I am still learning to believe. I never meditate upon any article of the Creed without some fresh learning to believe. The same is true when I meditate upon any passage in the Bible.

Meditation is that exercise in which the mind is directed toward growth in the wisdom of the heart and the understanding of the soul. It is the activity which alone enables us to grow in wisdom and knowledge and love toward God.

Creedal meditation is actually biblical meditation, for the Creed is the salvation-history of the Bible in synopsis. It keeps sending us back constantly to the Bible. But no meditation fit to be called Christian can end up in the Bible; it must end up somewhere in the world. No meditation is finished until it has gone forth from the sanctuary of our private chamber into the street. Christian meditation is the contemplation of the works of Christ, resulting in both vision and action. It makes things happen. If it does not make things happen, it is only sanctimonious woolgathering. By its fruits in action you shall know it, whether it be of God. Of course, the result of meditation need not always be some outward action on our part; it may be a change in our own heart and will, making us more like Christ within.

All Christian meditation begins with one question and ends with another. It begins: "Lord, what do you want me to see?" It ends: "Lord, what do you want me to do?" I have already quoted two great Victorians. Another, William E. Gladstone, said this: "There is one proposition which the experience of life burns into my soul; it is this, that a man should beware of letting his religion spoil his morality. In a thousand ways, some great, some small, but all subtle, we are daily tempted to that great sin."

With the heart, says Paul, a person believes and so grows in grace, goodness, and life (Romans 10:10). This belief of the heart, as distinguished from opinion of the head, is nourished by love. About this too Mr. Gladstone had a good word for us: "Many men know their opinions, few their convictions; but in the long run convictions rule, opinions go to the wall." A conviction is a heart-belief. It cannot contradict the mind and live; it must seem sound and right to the reason. But what vitalizes it is a compound of faith, love, loyalty, and commitment to its object. An opinion is simply a thought or an idea in mind which at the moment prevails over rival options.

For the believing Christian the articles of the Creed are convictions, not opinions. By them he "learns to believe" in God, and this learning is a lifelong growth in loving intimacy with God. It comes from following Jesus in love and obedience, meditating upon him as we go. He is the subject of all Christian meditation. Our meditation enables him to do his work with us and through us. It is loving the Lord with our minds. Christ himself is our creed, and our meditation is doing what it is meant to do when it enables us to see him more clearly, love him more dearly, follow him more nearly.

> Let the words of my mouth and the meditation of my heart, be alway acceptable in thy sight, O Lord, my strength, and my redeemer.
>
> Psalm 19:14

2

One God, One World

The whole difference between construction and creation is exactly this: that a thing constructed can only be loved after it is constructed; but a thing created is loved before it exists.

G. K. Chesterton,
Preface to Dickens's *Pickwick Papers*

It has been well said that Christianity began as a trinitarian religion with a unitarian theology. Jesus, with his fellow Jews, saw God as one, not several. His creed was the *Shema*: "Hear, O Israel: the Lord our God is one Lord" (Deuteronomy 6:4). He lived and died by this creed, would never have dreamed of altering it by a jot; and in fact he did not alter it, nor did his Church in later times. The Old Israel's proclamation that God is one is repeated by the New Israel, the Church.

The first Christians knew themselves as children of one Father, but they saw the Father through his Son Jesus, who was their human friend and brother. They were given to understand that to love and serve Jesus was to love and serve the Father. Thus in their experience there were these two distinct dimensions of Deity—the Father and the Son.

Then there was the experience associated with Pentecost (Acts 2). After that, and as a result of it, Christians knew that they lived in—and were lived in by—One whom they variously called the Spirit, the Holy Spirit, the Spirit of God, the Spirit of Christ—and Christ. For a time they used the words "Spirit" and "Christ" interchangeably. The Spirit was God in them, and in whom they lived.

Such was the trinitarian religion of the earliest Christians. Theology always comes after religion, literally as an afterthought. Men first experience God, then reflect upon their experience, and that reflection is their theology.

In the ancient world were "gods many and lords many." The Jewish and Christian proclamation that God is one was so revolutionary that it earned for both Jews and Christians the reputation of being atheists. The popular reasoning was that people who believe in only one God can hardly be said to believe in Deity at all. That thought-world is long dead. Not many today seriously wonder whether God is one or several; the modern question is whether he is one or none.

The unity of God is not simply a matter of numerical oneness. It means God's absolute sovereignty. As the source of all being, all reality, all life, God is alone; he does not share his glory with any other. In her *Last Lines* Emily Brontë captures the wonder of this truth:

> With wide-embracing love
> Thy Spirit animates eternal years,
>   Pervades and broods above,
> Changes, sustains, dissolves, creates, and rears.
>
>   Though earth and man were gone,
> And suns and universes ceased to be,
>   And Thou were left alone,
> Every existence would exist in Thee.

To say that God is alone in his sovereignty is not to say that he is lonely. A person is lonely when he lacks companionship, but God lacks nothing. His aloneness is that of the only Source of all that exists. He has no peers to be his companions, but he has all his creatures in which to delight. God could not conceivably be "left alone," since "every existence would exist" in him. He creates a world for himself to love, not because he is lonely, but because he is Love; and to love is to give.

That is why you and I are here, and every other creature: to be loved by God. As Chesterton has reminded us, we are not constructed—we are created.

We moderns habitually misuse the word "creative" as applied to human beings. It's a nice question, indeed, whether we ought ever to call anybody "creative" except God. Creation is the gift of being to nonbeing. God creates "out of nothing," and clearly no human being can do that. At most, you or I can be an instrument whom God uses for the creating and building up of others. By being faithful servants (which always consists of being lovers in God's image), we participate instrumentally in God's work of creation.

All creation comes from the one Hand; therefore, all creation is one—a *uni*verse. The Old Testament Hebrews did not develop a philosophical belief about the cosmos. Neither, for that matter, did the New Testament Christians. They assumed, rather than argued, that the world of the one God is one world. But as the new faith moved out into the gentile world, it picked up the philosophical habit of asking the why, whence, and wherefore of the things believed on faith. The Church Fathers related the unity of God to the unity of his world. They taught us that to say "I believe in one God" is to say that there is nothing in the whole universe that God does not create, over which he does not rule, and for our treatment of which we are not accountable to him.

The Christian mind of Francis Thompson was haunted, as every Christian mind ought to be, by the implications for our living of the unity of God's world. In "The Mistress of Vision" he wrote:

All things by immortal power,
Near or far,
Hiddenly
To each other linkèd are,
That thou canst not stir a flower
Without troubling of a star.

If, in this world as it is, I cannot stir a flower without troubling of a star, I must handle flowers reverently—and human beings more so.

The living unity of all things under God has been revealed to other than Christians. Three centuries before Christ the Chinese sage Chuang-tzu declared: "Tao is in the ant, in the broken tile, in dung, in mire." (*Tao* in Chinese means roughly what *logos* means in Greek; its presence betokens the presence of the Divine.) And the Vedanta asks: "Is not everything Brahman when the name and the form have been removed from it?" Brahman is the divine reality. Such expressions from nonbiblical religions bespeak a strong awareness of the unity of all things in God.

This metaphysical truth is also a moral mandate. It is a spiritual kinship that needs to be powerfully, even compulsively felt. Francis Thompson felt it when he spoke of troubling stars by stirring flowers. Eugene V. Debs, the socialist saint, felt it. In September 1918 he was convicted of conspiring against civil order, and he addressed to the judge these words: "Your honor, years ago I recognized my kinship with all living things, and I made up my mind that I was not one whit better than the meanest of earth. I said then, I say now, that while there is a lower class, I am of it; while there is a criminal element, I am of it; while there is a soul in prison, I am not free."

God's relationship to his world is sometimes compared to an author's relationship to a story he has written. The author creates his characters and then controls their action. Ideally, he has his mind on everybody and everything in his story all at once. Actually, he falls far short of this. In Dickens's novels, for example, we constantly see evidence of his inability to coordinate and unify perfectly all the details of his story. Dickens would be the first to complain that his characters are always getting out of hand. The divine Author, by contrast, does perfectly with his creation what the human author vainly aspires to do.

When Chesterton was still a schoolboy, he wrote about a book he had read: "What I like about this novelist is that he takes such trouble about his minor characters." To the eye of faith it is a matter for unceasing wonder, love, and praise how the divine Author "takes such trouble about his minor characters"—human and other. As I have seen written somewhere: "Even the sparrow is a cheeky little someone to God." This we need not only to believe, but to *feel* most steadily and intensely—and to live by that feeling.

> Greater still, Lord, let your universe be greater still, so that I may hold You and be held by You by a ceaselessly widened and intensified contact!
>
> Pierre Teilhard de Chardin,
> *The Divine Milieu*

3
Abba

My little son, who looked from thoughtful eyes
And moved and spoke in quiet grown-up wise,
Having my law the seventh time disobeyed,
I struck him, and dismissed
With hard words and unkissed,
His mother, who was patient, being dead.
Then, fearing lest his grief should hinder sleep,
I visited his bed,
But found him slumbering deep,
With darkened eyelids, and their lashes yet
From his late sobbing wet.
And I, with moan,
Kissing away his tears, left others of my own;
For, on a table drawn beside his head,
He had put, within his reach,
A box of counters and a red-veined stone,
A piece of glass abraded by the beach
And six or seven shells,
A bottle with bluebells
And two French copper coins, ranged there with
   careful art,
To comfort his sad heart.
So when that night I prayed
To God, I wept, and said:
Ah, when at last we lie with trancèd breath,
Not vexing Thee in death,
And Thou rememberest of what toys
We made our joys,
How weakly understood,
Thy great commanded good,
Then, fatherly not less
Than I whom Thou hast moulded from the clay,
Thou'lt leave Thy wrath, and say,
"I will be sorry for their childishness."

Coventry Patmore, "The Toys"

It is a sign of holy health in us that we should feel a living kinship with all of nature: that is, with all that lives and grows; but this must not make us nature-worshipers. We are a part of nature, and with the rest of nature we belong to the God who creates and rules us. The Italian poet Giacomo Leopardi a century ago was annoyed by the sentimental romantic naturalism of his contemporaries and protested that "Nature gives us life like a mother but loves us like a stepmother." He was only a little closer to the truth than they were. The love we receive, whether motherly or stepmotherly, is not from nature but from nature's God, of whom Paul tells us that he has "sent forth the Spirit of his Son into our hearts, crying, 'Abba! Father!'" (Galatians 4:6).

Abba is one of those words, like *Amen* and *Alleluia*, which we have carried over bodily from the Hebrew (in this case Aramaic) because there is no real synonym in English. "Father" lacks the tone of intimate tenderness with which *Abba* is charged. Some suggest that we translate it as "Daddy." I hope I'm not just being stuffy when I resist this. In our idiom "Daddy" does, to be sure, express affection, but it fails to express respect and filial fear.

Jesus used the word *Abba* in a way that revolutionized our way of thinking about God. In his agony in Gethsemane he cried, "Abba, Father, all things are possible to thee" (Mark 14:36). What an awesome text! Christ is never more human than when he sweats blood in his death anguish. Yet even then he speaks to God in this tenderest of terms—*Abba*.

To be sure, Jesus was by no means the first to use the word. Normally the Jew of his day used it in addressing his human father. But when he spoke of his divine Father he used the formal and nonintimate *Abi* ("my father") or *Abinu* ("our father"). When Jesus cried *Abba* in prayer, he asserted a closer relationship to God than any man had ever claimed before.

But that was not all. Not only did he himself call God *Abba*, he taught his disciples to do so. After they had received his Spirit, they addressed God as *Abba*. Being in Christ and in the Spirit, they now saw themselves as "sons in the Son" (Augustine's phrase). What Christ was to the Father so were they—in Christ—to the Father. *Abba* said it all—and still does. In *The Parables of Jesus*, Joachim Jeremias notes that from the Day of Pentecost to the present, "the first step in conversion and the new life is learning how to call God Abba with childlike confidence, safe under his protection and conscious of his boundless love."

God is *Abba* before he is maker of heaven and earth: that is, his father-love is the premise of his power and sovereignty. The good news of the gospel is that God is *Abba*. The gospel is good news about God, not good news about Jesus; it is the good news *of* Jesus, that God is *Abba*. Augustine well said in a sermon (no. 213): "*I believe in God the Father Almighty*. See how quickly it is said and how much it signifies! God exists and he is the Father: God by his power, Father by his goodness."

Because nowadays we commonly deplore paternalism, we must ask: Is God's dealing with his children paternalistic? "The black man is fed up with the white man's paternalism." "I'm against a paternalistic welfare-state government." Paternalism is commonly assumed to be a benevolent but misguided way of treating mature people as childish: a paternalistic person or government is Big Daddy.

Undeniably, many Christians of every age have thought of God in daddy-like terms, approaching him in the belief that he might prove a soft touch if handled rightly. They have been able to quote some New Testament texts which at first blush seem to support their case; for example, this promise of Jesus: "Whatever you ask of the Father in my name he will give you" (John 16:23). This seems to say that, if we want something badly enough and we ask God for it, he is bound to deliver. If this were true, God's world would be the most totally paternalistic "welfare state" imaginable, which quite obviously it is not. But the governing phrase in our Lord's promise is "in my name." To pray in Christ's name is to pray as a member of Christ, in Christ's person, in Christ's place, with Christ's mind—the mind that wants only what God wants. And the promise is literally true: when we do that, we get fully and exactly what we ask for. When Jesus prayed in Gethsemane, he asked for what the Father wanted—nothing less, or more, or other. To pray in his name is to pray like that; and clearly there is no "paternalism" in such praying or in God's response to it.

I once heard Dr. Paul Scherer declare in a sermon: "God's love isn't soft as mush; it's hard as nails." God is *Abba*; he is not Big Daddy. A Big-Daddy God would never ask us to take up crosses.

Because of the parrot-fashion way in which most Christians recite the Lord's Prayer, the fatherhood of God has become for many a mere pious phrase. What we easily forget about our filial relationship with God is that we have a natural enmity against God which must be overcome before we can know him as *Abba*. Alfred North Whitehead had this in mind when he wrote in *Religion in the Making* that religion "runs through three stages, if it evolves to its final satisfaction. It is the transition from God the void to God the enemy, and from God the enemy to God the companion."

Whatever our life with God may have been before the Fall, as we are now we start with God the Void: nothing there at all. Then, collectively if not always individually, we experience enmity against God as the troubler of our peace and the determiner of our destiny, which we would much prefer to determine for ourselves: God the Enemy. Only by the power of God the Spirit working in us can we finally come to the vision, knowledge, and love of God as *Abba*.

Paul felt that he had to warn Christians that no one can say that Jesus is Lord, but by the Holy Spirit (1 Corinthians 12:3). Likewise, no one can call God *Abba* except by the Spirit who is the Spirit of adoption. The Spirit who makes us children of the Father by adoption and grace bestows upon us the great sevenfold gift: "the spirit of wisdom and understanding, the spirit of counsel and ghostly strength, the spirit of knowledge and true godliness . . . and the spirit of . . . holy fear."*

The modern Christian may well lift an eyebrow at "holy fear." For isn't love supposed to cast out fear? Has not Christ set us free from bondage to fear? This sadly neglected subject needs careful understanding. There are not only differing degrees of fear but differing kinds of fear. There is servile fear, the fear of a slave for a cruel master. Then there is holy fear, or filial fear, which Francis J. Hall in his *Dogmatic Theology* defined as "loving anxiety to please God." Many years ago, in a book entitled *Living the Lord's Prayer,* I said something that I would here repeat without alteration: "There is a difference between fearing God and being afraid of him. . . . To fear God is to stand in awe of him; to be afraid of God is to run away from him." The filial fear, which belongs to the sevenfold gift of the Spirit, is awe of God, reverence, and loving anxiety to please him. Filial fear is childlike love of God, the love that cries *Abba.* When our sense of being God's dear children is strong enough to give us a real dread of disappointing him and disgracing the good name of the holy family into which we have been adopted, then—and only then—are we beginning to love God as we ought; we are beginning to know him as *Abba.*

> O most loving Father, who willest us to give thanks for all things, to dread nothing but the loss of thee, and to cast all our care on thee, who carest for us; Preserve us from faithless fears and worldly anxieties, and grant that no clouds of this mortal life may hide from us the light of that love which is immortal, and which thou hast manifested unto us in thy Son, Jesus Christ our Lord.
>
> *The Book of Common Prayer*

---

*In the traditional Anglican rite of Confirmation.

4

The Father Almighty

The ministering angels wanted to sing a hymn at
the destruction of the Egyptians, but God said:
"My children lie drowned in the sea, and you
would sing?"

Jewish legend

We believe in the almighty, the omnipotent Father; yet it is
seriously questionable whether these adjectives have done
more good than harm to our understanding of God. Somehow the *omni*—"all"—part of the word has determined our
basic concept rather than the *potens*—"mighty"—part of it.
God's omnipotence is commonly taken to mean that God can
do any and all things whatever. From this premise it is easy to
conclude that God can do things that we should call evil if a
man were to do them. If God can "do anything," he can
change his mind about us, break his promises, switch from
loving to hating his creatures. The powerful man is he who
can "throw his weight around" without hindrance from anybody; must not the powerful God be like that, only infinitely
more so? Words like "omnipotent" seem to trigger such reasoning about God. The resulting theology is sub-Christian.

Our thinking about God's power best begins at Calvary,
where we see that power as preeminently the power of self-
giving love. Whatever Jesus did and was in his human ministry, God does and is in his eternal ministry. The words and
works of Jesus are the words and works of the Divine Omnipotence "scaled down" in such a way that we can see and hear
them. Jesus called children to himself and blessed them. From
this we know that God loves and blesses children with
fatherly delight in them.

In him who for our sake became poor, we meet the almighty and eternal God. All power, all freedom are in the man Christ Jesus. He has all power to do for himself what fallen creatures daydream of doing for themselves—if only they could: "If I were God, I should take what I want, do what I want; but alas, lacking God's omnipotence, I must resign myself to my own impotence." Such reasoning reveals total ignorance of God's nature and power.

If Christ's power is God's power, *Omnipotence is Love.* God's love is his omnipotence in action. Pure love is omnipotent because it will unfailingly accomplish whatever it sets out to do. But how do we know this? There is no logic, no means of demonstration, by which it can be proved to others. It is only by our own participation in this divine mystery that we learn its secret. Christianity is in truth the supreme mystery-religion: only by loving as Christ loves is one initiated into the power of love. The living member of Christ is an instrument of the love of God. "And though I . . . understand all mysteries, and all knowledge . . . and have not love, I am nothing" (1 Corinthians 13:2). To those who believe, and express their belief by loving action, the cross of Christ is the very power of God (1 Corinthians 1:18). The cross is love in action, and its power never finally fails in its undertakings. Its apparent failures are only setbacks and delays. If the true test of power is the ability to create, that love which is the power of God is ultimately the only power there is.

Only love can create. This may be hard to accept as the whole truth of the matter, just as it stands. What are we to say of the empire-builder driven by greed and lust for power who "creates" for himself an empire by hook, crook, sweat, luck, and ruthless disregard for other people? Greed, not love, has wrought this monster. But because it is a monster, it is not a true creation. It cannot be assimilated to God's true creation around it, and it will not last. Such an empire shares the destiny of that of the Canaanite generalissimo we read about in chapters 4 and 5 of the Book of Judges. The biblical poet gives him this epitaph: "They fought from heaven; the stars in their courses fought against Sisera."

Human history as written by human beings teaches theology only very indirectly, and as commentary; but to the discerning student of human events it becomes clear that anything in this world that is built by any power other than love has in its cornerstone the seed of its own destruction.

God's power and love are one. With this in mind let us consider a problem about our theology which has come to the fore in our day. When we speak of our Father in heaven, we seem to be speaking of God as an individual being—a supreme being, no doubt, but nonetheless *a* being among other beings. He is "up there" or "out there" while we are "down here." He is an inconceivably greater being than we are. But if we, his creatures, are beings in our own right, and God is another being in his own right, it can hardly be said that there is none other beside him. If God is a being along with other beings, he does not have *sovereign* power and dominion. People who think about God in this way, as a supreme being over inferior beings, may question or doubt that he has the *power* to do what his *love* may will to do. May not evil or stupid inferior beings frustrate the will of the supreme being?

That problem arises out of a false theology. God is not *a* being, not even a supreme being: he is the Source, the Ground, the Giver of all being. Strictly speaking, God does not exist; for to exist (from Latin *ex-sisto*) is to come forth, appear, be projected from one's original ground. God is the ground from whom all beings exist, come forth; hence he is self-subsistent rather than existent. If God were a being, an existent, he would bear the limitations of derivativeness and contingency which belong to all existent creatures. This is what some theologians have in mind when they say that God cannot exist as "the supreme being" or "the divine person."

On this point they are entirely orthodox. Nobody will accuse Paul of unorthodoxy. He proclaims to the Athenians the God in whom "we live, and move, and have our being" (Acts 17:28). If we have our being in him and from him, God is not another individual being; he is Being—the Ground of all that exists.

But once we have seen this distinction between divine Being and human beings, we must ask: If God is not an individual personal being, how can he be our Father and how can we be his children? The question is about the meaning of personality. To be a person is to have a mind capable of decision and a will capable of action: that is the difference between a person and a thing. A thing cannot act; it can only be acted upon. To be personal is to be capable of rational and voluntary action. It is not the same thing as to be alive. A tree is alive, but not personal; it lives by passive reaction to the nutritive forces acting upon it from outside itself. And these nutritive forces are not personal, even though they "act"; for they do not act on their own initiative.

Personality is the ability to think, will, and act freely as one chooses. There are degrees and levels of personality. What makes some people more personal than others is their greater freedom, the fruit of their greater love. To send a man to prison is to deprive him of much of his freedom and thus to reduce his capacity to be personal. An alcoholic or any other addict lacks the freedom to determine his conduct, and so is less a person than he would be if he were free. Personality is functional freedom. The saint is the most personal of people because the most free, being the least curbed and crippled by self-concern. To be fully personal is to be fully free to love. Our alcoholic friend may be a father who, in his heart, loves his children, but it would be more accurate to say that he *wishes he could* love his children. He wishes he could give them his best and his all; but his wish, though loving, is only a wish. It cannot become an efficacious will until he is freed from his bondage.

Only God is perfectly personal because only he is perfectly loving. His perfect love is perfect power to create. If we have in us any of this creative power which is love, it is not really ours but God's power working through us. And this answers the question we raised earlier: If God is not an individual personal being, how can he be our Father and how can we be his children? The bond between a human father and his child is the bond between two creatures, an older one and a younger, both of them derivative beings from God, each of them only partially personal. The bond between God the Father and his child is the bond between the Creator and his creature whom his love has called into being out of nothing. And we show ourselves children of our Father, as Jesus teaches us, by doing the Father's will—which always consists of being agents of his love and instruments of his peace.

> O Lord, our Christ, may we have thy mind and thy spirit; make us instruments of thy peace; where there is hatred, let us sow love; where there is injury, pardon; where there is discord, union; where there is doubt, faith; where there is despair, hope; where there is darkness, light; and where there is sadness, joy.
>
> O divine Master, grant that we may not so much seek to be consoled as to console; to be understood as to understand; to be loved as to love; for it is in giving that we receive; it is in pardoning that we are pardoned; and it is in dying that we are born to eternal life.
>
> Prayer of St. Francis of Assisi

5

God's Agenda

Whatever weaknesses, miscalculations, and guilt
there are in what precedes the facts, God is in the
facts themselves.

Dietrich Bonhoeffer,
Letters and Papers from Prison

In the beginning God *began to create* the heavens and the
earth: this is the purport of the creation saga in Genesis. God
began what he has been doing ever since. The Bible makes
several cardinal affirmations such as these: God alone creates
the whole universe (and not just what we consider the "good
parts" of it). He created the physical structure of the world—
at any rate of this planet—before placing life in it. Before his
human creature appeared, God blessed his creation and
called it good. Finally, he made our first parent as a special
and unique being, forming him of earthly matter like other
animals but also making him in his own image and likeness as
a spiritual being.

This creation story is prescientific, but about this something very important needs to be understood: Genesis makes
scientific thought possible. We should never have dreamed of
studying our world scientifically unless we had had a prior
conviction that it makes sense and therefore *can* be studied.
Science as the systematic study of reality has flourished only
on cultural soil fertilized by biblical religion. Genesis is not
geology, but it makes geology possible by planting in the
minds of potential geologists the intuition that their enter-
prise makes sense because its laboratory is a world that
makes sense. Jews and Christians, as taught by the Bible, are

sure that every item, every phenomenon in this world is intelligible to the mind able to grasp it, because all is the expression of a divine and perfect Intelligence. As Bonhoeffer declares in our text for this meditation, "God is in the facts themselves"—all of them.

Most people, however, are not so much troubled by fear that the world may not make rational sense as by the fear that it may not make moral sense. It is one thing to believe that God is Perfect Intelligence so that all that he makes and does is intelligible. It is quite another thing to trust that he is Pure Love, that he cares for his creatures as a father cares for his children. Genesis proclaims that God finds all that he has made very good. Every sane person hopes that it is, but many ask with anxious wonder: If God has made all things bright and beautiful, whence comes the ugliness that we find both inside and outside ourselves?

When I meditate upon this dark mystery, an old folk saying comes to mind: "Dirt is misplaced soil." Dirt is "dirty" only when not in its right place. Dirt is soil, and from soil comes our daily bread, from soil comes man himself. If dirt is misplaced soil, may not bad things be good things misplaced?

Certainly we live in a very dirty world. Its dirt may be good things out of their right places; but, because there is so much of it, a large part of the work of God and his human junior partner must consist in putting it all back into its right place. Much good science is directed toward restoring "dirt" to its primal state as "soil." The right use of anything is that which is life-enhancing; the wrong use is that which hurts or destroys life. Some germ causes a disease and so is a dirty creature. If we can learn how to use this germ in some life-saving serum, the dirt becomes soil.

Or consider our inveterate savagery as the human race. In *The Decline and Fall of the Roman Empire*, Edward Gibbon gave it as his considered judgment that history is "little more than the register of the crimes, follies, and misfortunes of mankind." If we are so constructed that we cannot behave otherwise, we are doomed to an ever-darkening future. William James was groping toward a more hopeful answer when he spoke of our need for a "moral equivalent of war." He wasn't dreaming of some kind of psychic castration that would remove our aggressive impulses; he was thinking, rather, of finding the right channels for these drives. Dr. Frank Laubach had all of Napoleon's passion for world conquest. He worked for more than half a century at the conquest of illiteracy throughout the world. His achievement was prodigious, but his career has a value and meaning entirely apart from his work: here was a man in whom aggressiveness worked, not as life-destroying dirt, but as life-enhancing energy.

God creates the physical setting, then vegetable life, then animal life, and—finally—us. Through all this it is affirmed that God's world is truly one, a universe. The hidden gem in the dark ocean cave, the toad, the beautiful child, the criminal, the remotest star in the Milky Way, are all creatures of the Pure Love who is Pure Act. God blessed his creation and called it good before we as a species were born, and herein is healthy admonition for the human ego if we have the wisdom to receive it. We easily assume that, because we are apparently the crown of creation, we alone make the world precious to God; but according to Genesis the world was getting along very well in God's sight before us, and so it conceivably could after us. Nevertheless, God has a high destiny for us. In fashioning us from soil, he made us of a piece with other animals, but then he said: "Let us make man in our image, after our likeness: and let them have dominion over the fish of the sea, and over all the fowl of the air, and over the cattle, and over the earth, and over every creeping thing that creepeth upon the earth" (Genesis 1:26).

God speaks of himself plurally. This may be understood as the plural of majesty, like a king or a pope referring to himself as "we," or it may be a lingering echo of polytheism in the Hebrew language. Christians, however, have seen here a revelatory allusion to the triunity of God's being: it is the One God in Three Persons who creates the world. John Donne preached on this text "Let us make" and said: "It was the entertainment of God himself, his delight, his contemplation, for those infinite millions of generations when he was without a world, without creatures, to joy in one another, in the Trinity. It was the Father's delight to look upon himself in the Son; and to see the whole Godhead, in a threefold and an equal glory." Christians loving God for what he is in himself find his joyful self-sufficiency a subject for adoring contemplation, and also a truth germane to a sound view of creation: that God creates us with a capacity for sharing with him his loving delight in himself and in all that he is, and makes, and does.

We are created in God's sublime image. We can make rational decisions, can consciously change the world around us, can love, can sin, and can weep for our sins. If the first chapter of Genesis contained the whole story of our human family from the beginning until now, we could happily declaim with Hamlet: "What a piece of work is a man! How noble in reason! how infinite in faculty! in form, in moving, how express and admirable! in action how like an angel! in apprehension how like a god! the beauty of the world! the paragon of animals!" But alas, in life as in Genesis, chapter 1 is only the beginning.

In chapter 2, in Genesis and in life, we fall out of harmony and partnership with God. The Christian creed does not mention the Fall by name, but it doesn't need to, for our alienation from God and from our selves is the backdrop of all that is said in the Creed. If we were not fallen, there would be no need for us to declare our belief in God the Father Almighty, with all that follows from that, for we should then speak from a position not of faith but of sight, of vision. Adam before the Fall needs no faith; he speaks with God face-to-face. He needs no redemption, no Christ to rescue him.

Modernistic Christians skirt around the doctrine of the Fall. The truth which it expresses is obviously distasteful. Yet there is a more cheerful truth about it which we miss if we avoid the subject. This truth was spoken by an Anglican priest, Father Waggett, as he and his friend Gilbert Chesterton stood on the Mount of Olives in view of Gethsemane. After they had silently viewed the scene of Christ's agony, the priest remarked, "Well, anyhow, it must be obvious to anybody that the doctrine of the Fall is the only *cheerful* view of human life." I'm not sure it's obvious to anybody; it can be evident only to those who ponder it deeply, with contrition and faith. The cheerful truth about it is that any creature who can cause such distress in high heaven as we do by our rebellion against our Father must be a creature most dear, and most important, to God.

Years ago I read somebody's statement that he doesn't believe in hell because he doesn't believe we are "worth a damn" to God. That is how people are likely to think about us if they have no conviction of both the terrible Fall and the glorious Redemption. The Creed is really all about this "cheerful" doctrine—cheerful for two reasons: it reveals our high dignity as God's children, and it reveals the unfathomable love of God who thinks us not only "worth a damn" but worth the highest price that even God can pay to reclaim us for himself.

> Create in me a clean heart, O God; and renew a right spirit within me.
>
> Psalm 51:10

6

The Preparation of the Gospel

History is God's roaring loom.

J. S. Whale

According to the best informed guesses, the human race has been on this planet for about a million years. We are late-comers compared to some lizards and insects, and the planet itself is millions of years older than we are. Let us scale down this million years to twenty-four hours and imagine that we are standing at midnight. Looking back over the day, we see that Christianity broke into the news at about 11:57 P.M. The birth in Bethlehem came too late to make the early edition of tomorrow morning's newspaper. Taking the whole sweep of history into account, one might reasonably conclude that Christianity is too new a factor in history to have much of a track record, either good or bad, since it has barely got started.

Another thought arises. If Christ, the healer of our sick race, began his work only three minutes ago, what can be said for the goodness of a God who would let his sick children go uncared for throughout the previous twenty-three hours and fifty-seven minutes (actually, a million years)?

The Christian answer is that Christ's saving work is not coterminous and coextensive with historical Christianity. From the beginning, Christ, who was in the beginning with God, has been the light of every man coming into the world (John 1:9). There never was a time when he was not shepherding the human flock which the Father had given into his care.

The term "preparation of the gospel" refers to all workings

of Christ in times or cultures or human situations which do not fall within the formally Christian dispensation. Wherever he is at work in life, it is to prepare for a fuller disclosure of himself. Human life is fallen everywhere. The sign of the Fall is always the same: our living for self rather than for God. And the sign of the presence of Christ is always the same: our striving to live for God and our neighbor. Where that is seen the Cross is seen, and we know that Christ is there.

For ages we have been comparing two great deaths, those of Socrates and Christ. Christians have seen in the great Athenian's martyrdom an antetype of the death of Christ. We may go beyond that and say that Christ was the Light who lightened Socrates in his living and in his dying. Four hundred years before the birth in Bethlehem Christ visited Socrates with that life which is the light of men (John 1:4), and so it need not surprise us that Socrates said with his blood what Jesus would say with his blood: that we should not fear him who can kill the body, but only him who can kill the soul.

Another example: Hinduism, the great indigenous religion of India, is predominantly polytheistic; but, at about the time the Christian era began, there was a development in Hinduism in which the god Vishnu came to be adored as the One God. In Hindu theology generally, there is no love relationship between God and man. In the Vishnu cult, however, there was a strong movement toward personal love for God. The seventeenth-century poet Tukaram expresses it in this hymn to Vishnu:

> You hold my hand and guide me wherever I go.
> While I love and lean on you, you bear my heavy burden.
> You give me always new hope, and lead me to a new world.

In each man I see a friend, in each encounter a kins-
man.
I play in your lovely world, O God, like a happy
child.
And everywhere, says Tuka now, your goodness is
outpoured.

That sounds like many a familiar Christian hymn. It
expresses a Christian view of God. It appears that Christ has
been here in the hearts and minds of these worshipers of
Vishnu.

Staunchly orthodox doctors of the Church have seen the
preparation of the gospel in the words of the sages and the
works of the heroes of pagan antiquity. Augustine tells how,
in his youth, he came upon Cicero's *Hortensius*. This book,
he recalls in his *Confessions*, "quite altered my affection,
turned my prayers to thyself, O Lord, and made me have
totally other purposes and desires." Clement of Alexandria in
Stromateis saw Greek philosophy as "a schoolmaster to bring
the Greek mind to Christ," even as Paul saw the Law of Israel
as a schoolmaster to prepare God's people for Christ (Galatians 3:24). He meant that Christ was the master, and the
holy law the lesson, in this pre-Christian preparation.

The most striking assertion in Paul's writings of the prein-
carnate Christ's saving activity on earth is this, in his first
letter to the Corinthians: "You should understand, my
brothers, that our ancestors were all under the pillar of cloud,
and all of them passed through the Red Sea; and so they all
received baptism into the fellowship of Moses in cloud and
sea. They all ate the same supernatural food, and all drank
the same supernatural drink; I mean, they all drank from the
supernatural rock that accompanied their travels—and that
rock was Christ" (1 Corinthians 10:1-4). Christ was the guid-
ing cloud to the Israelites by day, and their pillar of fire by
night, and their food and drink as they followed Moses

through the wilderness. He was their savior, though they knew him not by name.

The Old Testament is largely the story of God's people rebelling, disobeying, forsaking God but not being forsaken by him. Through it all, Christ was forming them into himself and forming himself in them. It was because Christ was hiddenly in them that the saints of the Old Dispensation could have such visions of God as this:

The Lord is compassionate and gracious, long-suffering and forever constant; he will not always be the accuser or nurse his anger for all time.

He has not treated us as our sins deserve or requited us for our misdeeds.

For as the heaven stands high above the earth, so his strong love stands high over all who fear him.

Psalm 103:8–11

Strictly speaking, Christians have no need, and no right, to speak of taking "their" Christ out into the world and giving him to all people. He does not belong to Christians, and they do not carry him; they belong to him, and he carries them. Wherever we go in this world, Christ is already there and has been there from the beginning—preparing his people for full participation in the life of his kingdom.

What advantage, then, does the Christian have? Much in every way. The conscious knowledge of Christ our Life is a much greater boon than any unconscious response to him can be. Earlier in this century a young woman in China was converted to the Christian faith, and she joyfully testified: "All my life I have known him, but now I know his Name!" When you receive an anonymous gift, you are grateful and you bless the name of the giver—or you would if you knew who he is. When you receive a gift from a known friend, you can give back love in a way that makes an incalculable difference.

There is what someone has called "an ugly and uncharitable twist" in the world: a wound that needs to be healed, a strife that needs to be turned into harmony. Christ has been at work throughout the world preparing all people and all creatures for life in his restored and perfected kingdom. (If the word "kingdom" presents any kind of block to your conception, think of it as "order.") That kingdom is the unimpeded and total rule of God, and it is the great promise of Christ. Most of us need to broaden our conception of God's kingdom to grasp its full scope and to see our own role as its citizens and servants. This is one of the great themes of Teilhard de Chardin. God gave him to our age to open our eyes anew to the majestic wholeness and all-embracingness of God's kingdom. The whole world—every *thing* as well as every *body*—is "in the works" and intended for glory. We badly err when we see God's kingdom as embracing only some, or even all, human beings and human life. The person who works to save streams from pollution is serving the kingdom just as is one who bestows his goods to feed the poor. God working through Christ is repossessing and transforming all the world in each and all of its parts. There will be streams and stones and lizards in the glorious kingdom along with angels, men, women, and children. In *The Phenomenon of Man*, Teilhard says: "For reasons of practical convenience and perhaps also of intellectual timidity, the City of God is too often described in pious works in conventional and purely moral terms. God and the world he governs are seen as a vast association, essentially legalistic in its nature, conceived in terms of a family or government. The fundamental root from which the sap of Christianity has risen from the beginning and is nourished, is quite otherwise. Led astray by a false evangelism, people often think they are honoring Christianity when they reduce it to a sort of gentle philanthropism. Those who fail to see in it the most realistic and at the same time the most cosmic of beliefs and hopes, completely fail to understand its 'mysteries.' Is the Kingdom of God a big family? Yes, in a sense it is. But in another sense it is a prodigious biological operation—that of the Redeeming Incarnation" (p. 293).

To be sure, we—God's human creatures—are the key. Just as by us came the Fall which blighted our own life and that of all nature, so through us must come the redemption of nature by Christ the Lord. "Through him all *things* were made, and without him was not any *thing* made that was made" (John 1:3). Through him was made the wood on which he was crucified. And all things made through him are destined for glory in his restored kingdom: that is why they are here, in that preparation of the gospel which is the preparation of the world for his kingdom.

Whatever anybody does to enrich the life of this world is a service to Christ and his kingdom. Our Lord has countless hosts of good servants whom he knows though they know not him. The man who invented the wheel, the man who never cuts down a tree without replacing it—everybody who lays hands upon this world not to plunder and exploit but to serve and to save—are servants of him who is the Alpha, from whom all comes, and the Omega, toward whom all moves.

> O heavenly Father, who hast filled the world with beauty; Open, we beseech thee, our eyes to behold thy gracious hand in all thy works; that rejoicing in thy whole creation, we may learn to serve thee with gladness; for the sake of him by whom all things were made, thy Son, Jesus Christ our Lord.
>
> *The Book of Common Prayer*

7

The Descent of the Lover

> The Father is begetting his Son unceasingly, ar d
> furthermore he begets me his Son, his very own
> Son.
>
> Meister Eckhart

Robinson Jeffers wrote in "The Coast-Range Christ":

God was a hawk in the glow of the morning, a bee in the
    rose that has stars for her petals,
The far lights felt him, the first-born lamps
Spun from the brush of his wings when he bathed in the
    splendor of a firmament men's eyes never imaged,
Exulting in the beauty of things, a free eagle.
But love drew him dustward, for love's sake he stooped, like
    a lover came God with a garland of suns
In his locks and the wild wine freedom on his lips
To the earth and the arms of a Jewess, and to house with a
    tribe of tame serpents in the handmaiden planet
Of a least of the stars—the descent of the lover.

The gospel is the story of the descent of the Lover. Love
drew him dustward, and his love is the love of God. His
descent is the bringing of God's power and life to our world:
"As many as received him, to them gave he power to become
the sons of God" (John 1:12). The Greek myth of Pro-
metheus's bringing fire to man is a powerful representation of
truth that is fulfilled in Christ.

He comes into our life from the Ground of all being: from
"above" but also from "within." Matthew opens his Gospel

with the family tree of Jesus. It contains some great people but also some notorious sinners, such as Rahab, the whore and traitress; David, the murderer and adulterer; Solomon, the vain peacock who needed a thousand women; and Rehoboam, whose arrogant folly ruined a kingdom. Jesus comes out of human history as well as into it: into it from his heavenly Father, out of it from his earthly mother.

The divine Lover sees our race sick with the poisons of hate, fear, and that alienation from God which is always alienation from self. His love draws him dustward with a longing so to draw us into his own being that his life can be our life. This longing for love-union explains the metaphor of Christ as the bridegroom and his people as his bride. His coming down is like that coming down of the strong to the weak, the living to the dying. Life stands over death as do truth over falsehood, beauty over ugliness, love over hate, wisdom over folly. The strong person who loves the weak must always come down to the weak. The men who wrote the New Testament and those who later wrote the Creeds used this metaphor of coming down because it seemed most natural, and it still does.

He was conceived by the Holy Ghost and born of the Virgin Mary. The Virgin Birth is a sign from heaven, and biblically a sign is (a) an actual event and (b) an event that signifies something. Christ comes into our life in space-time to show us the Father. It was fitting that his heavenly Father should be his only father; for, if he had been the son of a human father, we might easily have supposed that his devotion to his "Father in heaven" was only a projection of his own sentimental father-image. We want a "Friend-behind-phenomena" who is like us; ideally, he should be some kind of indulgent heavenly father—a Big Daddy, even bigger and nicer than the biggest and nicest human father. This kind of wish-projection was as old and as universal as humanity before Jesus came (and it still is).

Evidently Jesus never, except perhaps as a small child, saw himself as Joseph's son.* Undoubtedly he remembered Joseph as a kind, brave, faithful foster father. But when he speaks of his Father we know whom he means, and it is not Joseph or any other man.

The Virgin Birth has another meaning. As "the first-born of all creation" (Colossians 1:15) Christ is the beginning of a new human race. To be baptized into him is to be born into this new race. Our first birth, into human life, is indeed by the power of the Holy Spirit, since all life is given by that power alone. But this birth takes place through the joint agency of our human parents. In our second birth, into the new and eternal life in Christ, we are born of the Spirit—"conceived by the Holy Ghost"—and are made children of our Father in heaven by adoption and grace. In this second birth we are born, as Jesus was, "not of blood, nor of the will of the flesh, nor of the will of man, but of God" (John 1:13). The new race, in Christ, began in the womb of Mary by a supernatural act of God. From that moment to this, people have been born into this new race by the same supernatural act of God: birth by divine paternity.

Several years ago at the Christmas season I heard Paul Harvey tell this story:

A man of our own time and place, whom we may call Mr. Smith, was a fine man and had a lovely family, but he honestly did not believe in Christianity or the Christmas story. One Christmas Eve his wife and children were going to

---

*What other inference can we draw, for example, from his words and actions during his visit to the Temple as a boy? (Luke 2:41–51). Then there is the fact, which we have touched upon in chapter 3, that Jesus used the intimate term *Abba*, which other Jews used for their human fathers, when he spoke to, or about, his Father in heaven. It is hardly conceivable that if he had ever known Joseph as *Abba*, he would have used the same term—referring to God.

church and invited him to join them. He declined, feeling that it would be wrong for him to go through the motions of worshiping a Christ in whom he did not believe. So he stayed home.

Their house had a large picture window, and, soon after the family left, Mr. Smith heard a noise as of many objects banging against that window. He investigated and found that a flock of birds, flying together, had apparently struck the window and were now wounded, stunned, and lying on the ground, some already dead. He was a tenderhearted man and knew that all would soon die of the cold if he left them there on the ground. So what to do? He thought of a pony stable out behind the house—a perfect shelter if he could get them into it. So he took a flashlight and walked toward the stable, hoping that the poor creatures would know enough to follow the gleam; but they didn't. He took bread crumbs and sprinkled them in the right direction, but that didn't work. Meanwhile, their plight was growing worse in the bitter cold, and he was at his wit's end to know how to save them. He said to himself: "If only I could become one of them, so that I could get right in there and lead the way! Then they would follow me to life."

In that moment he realized what Christmas is all about, and the Incarnation, and Christ. Here he was, wishing that he could become a bird so that he could save the birds.

Human beings have some things in common with those birds. Like them, we often follow wrong lights and consequently rack ourselves up disastrously. The birds saw the light in the Smith home and headed full speed toward it. They didn't see the window against which they smashed themselves. We see a light that looks inviting, and we throw all caution to the winds as we fly toward it.

Jesus told some stories about people who see a false light in money. Their end is often ruin. The pursuit of happiness, or power, or popularity as an end in itself is likewise self-destructive. But people have another source of misery and self-injury: a mysterious disease with which (or perhaps into which) we are born and which becomes virulent before we have left childhood. Theologians have called it Original Sin. It's something that we have had from the beginning of our species, that nobody escapes, that is always with us, that underlies our worst troubles and distresses.

"We find ourselves out of sympathy with God from the start," as theologian E. J. Bicknell has put it (*Essays, Catholic and Critical*, edited by E. G. Selwyn). I ask myself: Why is it that if I choose to do something that God forbids, I can do it with ease and usually pleasure; but if I choose to do something I know to be pleasing to God, it usually requires of me hard effort, self-discipline, and that special help from God which we call grace? There can be only one answer: I am out of sympathy with God from the start. Where God ought to be in my heart, my sacred ego sits enthroned, the capital I, dictating everything, so that what I do—even the supposedly generous things—I do for myself. Paul reminds me that I can bestow all my goods to feed the poor and give my body to be burned, and yet have in me no charity, only self-love. Whatever I do "naturally and normally," as we say, I do for myself first, and then, perhaps, for God and others after me.

Suppose now that I see this in myself and recognize it as sick behavior. A sick person's awareness of his condition is a necessary first step toward healing, but only that. I cannot heal myself from this sickness. No human therapy can heal me. I am as helpless against it as were the birds against their ignorance about lights and windows.

If this radical sickness is to be cured, somebody who does not share it himself, but who shares our humanity, must come to us in the way that Mr. Smith wanted to go to the birds, as one of our own kind, and say to us: Follow me and I will lead you out of this sickness into health, out of what you now are into what God wills you to be.

The moment we begin to follow Jesus as Lord of our lives, a miracle begins to take place in us: we begin to be our true selves. In Dickens's *Christmas Carol*, after Scrooge has been reborn we feel that we are seeing the real Scrooge for the first time; the old Scrooge was his pre-self. As our Lord leads us on and we become more like him, we become more our true selves; he is saving us not simply from our sins but from Sin—the root of all particular sins: our self-centeredness.

What Mr. Smith could not do for the birds, Christ does for us—because he can.

> O holy Child of Bethlehem!
> Descend to us, we pray;
> Cast out our sin and enter in,
> Be born in us today.
>
> Phillips Brooks

8

Getting into the Act

Luf copuls god & manne.

Richard Rolle of Hampole

God is Pure Act, said Thomas Aquinas. God is Love, said John the Divine. They were saying the same thing. Love is action to create.

Of course, love is one of the most ambiguous of words, and we can't use it intelligibly unless we define our usage of it. Love is usually thought of in terms of personal union. A man loves a woman and seeks union with her. But there is another way of conceiving of love, and this is in terms of service to the beloved. The former is unitive love; the latter is creative love. The former seeks union with the beloved; the latter seeks to create the beloved.

Even when we are thinking as Christians, we usually define love as union between lover and beloved; but as Christians we need to see this union as one of the desirable fruits of love rather than as love itself. Union may result from love, and the lover always hopes that it will; but it doesn't always result, for the beloved may not return the love, and without mutuality there can be no union. The love of Christ, which we may call Christ-love (or by its New Testament word *agapé*), always aims at enriching and fulfilling the life of the beloved—at helping him to become more his true self. A happy union may be hoped for by the lover, and richly deserved; but if he doesn't get it, he goes on loving to the end.

To love anybody with this Christ-love is to help God in creating that person. Let's test this. You give a doll to a little girl and you say, "But I'm not trying to create this child—I leave that to God! I just want to give her some pleasure." In so doing, you find your loving act a pleasure to yourself. But also you are serving God's purpose of creating the child. In making her happy, you have enhanced her life—and permanently, forever. Giving is not only more blessed than receiving, it is often more fun; often, but not always. Creative loving can be costly and painful. He who wills the increase of another must be prepared for the decrease of himself. And the lover may have to endure the bitterest pain of all—the alienation and antagonism of the beloved. Every Christian should have a constant, instant recall of the Classic Case.

God is Love; to love is to create; God is Pure Act—the Love who creates all; and Christ comes to us from God to draw us into the Act. "To as many as received him he gave power to become the children of God" (John 1:12). He gives to his living members power to be instruments of God in creating people and things for the new world that is coming.

Christians must mix their metaphors freely to describe their life in Christ in all its richness. They are lost sheep who have been found, salt of the earth, soldiers of Christ, ministers of reconciliation, "poor, yet making many rich" (2 Corinthians 6:10). At the present time in salvation-history they need to see more clearly than in the past their calling as God's partners (in the sense of servants rather than colleagues) in the continuing work of creation. This calls for a break with our long-established conventional way of loving. We often think we are loving somebody when in fact we are only grappling him to us with hoops of emotional steel, trying to claim him as our own. No human being has any such possessive right over another. Too commonly parents who are selfishly possessive of their children are praised as being superlatively devoted. But the only true test of a parent's love is his devotion to bringing out the authentic flavor of the child's unique self rather than trying to mold him or her in the parental image or the family likeness. The loving parent should want his or her child to be different from himself or herself in the way that God has made the child different, and any parent who does not want that is either indifferent or is egotistically possessive rather than loving. Such possessiveness is well called smother-love, but be it noted that fathers no less than mothers can smother.

Christians in their loving are called to aim at the good of the beloved, and that good is always true self-fulfillment. This is to love as God loves; it is in fact God's love working through human agents. Some twenty years ago a childless couple whom I know adopted a child of three, knowing that she was mentally retarded. They were troubled by the thought that, if she were never adopted by people who would love her as their own, she would have no chance to develop her limited potentialities. They seemed to me to have no idea of how purely Christian they were being. They saw the child from God's viewpoint. God sees every person as one who has to be brought along, created, to full perfection. Uppermost in their minds was the child's need for what they could contribute toward her creation to completion. Theirs is pure Christ-love; they have been drawn into the Act.

Not only do we need to love, we also need to be loved ourselves and to be further created. And we are created as we serve God in his creating others. "We know that we have passed from death to life, because we love the brethren," John declares (1 John 3:14). "Knowledge puffs up, love builds up," says Paul (1 Corinthians 8:1). Loving can be painful and costly, but it never loses its joy. It was "for the joy that was set before him" that Jesus endured the cross (Hebrews 12:2). Spinoza defined joy as the passage from a lesser to a greater perfection. An essential part of joy is the sense of growing in life itself, from strength to strength: we know that we are passing from death to life when we love. In this progression is joy, the joy that characterizes all life in Christ.

Catherine of Siena, in the fourteenth century, was an

ardent lover of God and of human souls. Christ had drawn her into the Act, and she had become a proficient in it. But her formulation of the rule of loving strikes me as less than adequate: "The reason why God's servants love creatures so much is that they see how Christ loves them, and it is one of the properties of love to love what is loved by the person we love." This view envisions the Christian looking at Christ's love for his creatures and then trying to imitate it. There is a better way than this, and Catherine herself exemplified it. She was no mere imitator of Christ's loving; she was an agent of Christ's loving. My friends who adopted the retarded child were not consciously imitating Jesus; rather, the mind and heart of Jesus toward the child was in them, and he has been doing his work of creating her mostly through them. You may be curious to know how it is working out. I can't answer that question, nor can anybody else. The child, like all the rest of us, is now in the process of being created, and how it is all working out will not be seen until the Day of the Lord. Meanwhile, we know that she is being built up because we know that she is being creatively loved by Christ, through her foster parents, and that love never fails.

There is another question: How can we know what to give to somebody for his or her fulfillment? There is no prescriptive answer to this. Only God knows exactly what anyone needs, and we must so play our part in the Act that God can meet the need through us. We are to be agents of his love, not architects of his program. Yet we must always be making choices in dealing with others. It is futile to ask God to show us what he has in view as the final end—his perfected, completed creature; we couldn't "see" it, comprehend it, if he did. No one on earth has ever seen a completed human being (except those who saw Jesus in the flesh). We can only ask God to show us what to do so that our efforts will not get in his way. If our every word is spoken and our every deed done in a spirit of prayerful openness to the light of the Holy Spirit, we shall make few, if any, mistakes as God's creative agents. The right rule is the only one: habitual, constant openness to the Spirit.

God gives us reason and faith as tools for our work of love. Neither is infallible; but reason, though fallible, will save us from many false choices if we use it "for all we've got"— which we too seldom do. Faith moves us to think and plan relying on the Holy Spirit for guidance. Thus reason, diligently used, fired by faith and guided by the Spirit, raises the simplest soul to efficacious loving action.

When you have been drawn into the Act, you need to remember, in all your doubts and perplexities, that it was God who began the good work in you and who will also finish it (Philippians 1:6). When some work of love blows up in your face, you will hear the Voice within saying, "The end is not yet!" It never is. And the end is always God's, as is the beginning and the continuance.

> O God, by whom the meek are guided in judgment, and light riseth up in darkness for the godly: Grant us, in all our doubts and uncertainties, the grace to ask what thou wouldest have us to do, that the Spirit of Wisdom may save us from all false choices, and that in thy light we may see light, and in thy straight path may not stumble, through Jesus Christ our Lord.
>
> *The Book of Common Prayer*

9

Why Did Jesus Die?

A God on the cross! That is all my theology.

Jean Baptiste Lacordaire

He suffered under Pontius Pilate. Why? There are two major questions here. Why did good men, acting in good conscience, kill Jesus—or get him killed? And what good did it do us?

We can answer the first question easily if we don't mind answering it superficially. We can say that Jesus was simply a victim of reactionary malice; that by his rabble-rousing preaching and behavior he antagonized powerful leaders of the Establishment who resolved to get rid of him and succeeded. This theory appeals to all who long for a humanitarian reform of society and see Jesus as the great prophet of compassionate revolution. They are against contemporary social reactionaries, and they see the spiritual ancestors of those villains in the men who engineered the crucifixion of Jesus. They are fairly right about the crucifiers but entirely wrong about the Crucified, for Jesus was not a social revolutionary. He proclaimed a kingdom not of this world. The social, political revolutionist dreams of a good kingdom of this world to replace the present evil one. Jesus was tempted to go that route, to seek power over all the world by revolution, but he rejected it (Matthew 4:8–10).

The case of his enemies against him was not sociopolitical but religious, although, in order to get him crucified, they had to convince the Roman governor that Jesus was an insurrectionist. (Pilate doesn't seem to have taken this preposterous claim at all seriously. He let the execution proceed only to get its native agitators off his back.) The enemies of Jesus told the governor that this man was plotting against Caesar, but what they really had against him was, they were convinced, that he was in league with the Devil. That which Christians worship in Jesus as divine they resisted as demonic.

It may require of us some effort to understand this. Perhaps a good approach to the mystery is by way of this old Yiddish proverb: "If God lived on earth people would break his windows." Consider also a stupid thing that was done in Athens five centuries before Jesus—a thing that happens in one way or another universally and unendingly in human life. The Athenians had a ruler so eminently just that he was commonly known as Aristides the Just. One day the citizens voted to banish him. One of them explained his vote, and undoubtedly the vote of most others, by saying, "I just tired of hearing him called Aristides the Just." What they tired of, in truth, was not what Aristides was called but what Aristides was: a better man than they were. What got him into trouble with his neighbors was what got Jesus into trouble: People couldn't take him. There was in Jesus a terrifying something they could not fathom, could not master, could not endure. But they did not see this awful *numen* in him as divine: they saw it as demonic. One of them said it straight out: "Are we not right in saying that you have a devil in you?" (John 8:48).

"If God lived on earth people would break his windows."

Here let us recall the dictum of Whitehead quoted in chapter 3: "Religion is what the individual does with his own solitariness. It runs through three stages, if it evolves to its final satisfaction. It is the transition from God the void to God the enemy, and from God the enemy to God the companion." This statement contains several pertinent implications. One is that, before we experience God as our friend, we—normally, at least—experience him as our enemy. Some of God's holiest saints have confessed how God has had to reconcile them to himself in order to win them from bitter enmity to eternal friendship.

The men who killed Jesus met in him God the Enemy and reacted accordingly. But how could this be? He came in love, offering them pardon, peace, joy, and life. He did things that revealed his own perfect lovableness as a man. The way he drew children to himself; the delightful stories he told; his compassion for the sick, the outcast, the hopeless, the sinful; his gaiety, humor, genius for friendship—all his wonderful qualities warmed the world around him. How, then, is it conceivable that men shuddered at his approach and recoiled against God the Enemy in him? There is a difficulty of conception here, and I want to avoid oversimplifying. Someone has well said that Jesus did not get himself crucified by saying such things as "Consider the lilies of the field, how they grow"; he did it, rather, by saying such things as "Consider the thieves in the temple, how they steal!" His presence was (and still is) a troubling presence. It made men angry, but it also made them shudder.

Their anger is easily understandable. It is not difficult to make other people angry; even I can do it. But their shudders, their revulsion, were provoked by something else, and this was Jesus' constant and characteristic way of speaking and acting with the absoluteness of God. Consider one example, his cleansing of the Temple (Mark 11:15–18). Ethically, the money-changing activity which he attacked was defensible. It was not a racket—at least not an illegal racket. Worshipers were required to pay a Temple tax. Jesus did not attack this requirement. The currency exchange was a practical necessity because the tax had to be paid in Jewish coinage, and so worshipers with only Roman money in their wallets needed this service. But the exchangers charged a commission, and Jesus denounced this as sacrilegious banditry. No matter that the Temple authorities approved it as lawful, which meant that in legal fact it *was* lawful; Jesus acted with the absoluteness which is the sole prerogative of God. In this action, as in others, he seemed to be God the Enemy Incarnate who had come to destroy these law-abiding, God-fearing men.

Is the divine Enemy God or Devil? From the viewpoint of threatened people it makes no real difference whether this frightful adversary is God or Devil: he is the Devil-God; and they felt that the Devil-God was in Jesus. They hoped that, by killing Jesus, they could deprive God the Enemy of this terrible human voice, shape, and presence. Understandably, the people who had a bigger stake in the status quo tended to react more passionately against him, feeling that they had more to lose at the hands of the Devil-God. Jesus seemed, however, to threaten all sorts and conditions of men. He made them inexplicably, but painfully, uncomfortable. Simply by being there where they could see him, he convicted them of falling short in their own being. He had a daily beauty in his life that made them ugly. It has been so ever since. His purity condemns our lusts; his beauty makes us ugly. In him we see the Judge, the Troubler of our peace, the Enemy; and his effect upon those who encountered him "in the raw" must have been devastating.

He came to his own, and his own received him not. They could not see that he had come, not to destroy, but to save. God had to be seen as enemy before he could be seen as friend. When God lived on earth, we had to smash his windows. When God stands between us and the desires of our childish and selfish hearts, he appears as the great Nay-sayer to our happiness. His word must be heard as judgment before it can be heard as grace.

Any honest soul knows all this from his own self-knowledge. When a Christian knows what God asks of him but his heart is fixed upon some other goal, the Lord confronts him as the Enemy; Christ speaks to him as the accuser. The Holy Spirit must show the person caught in this conflict that the word of judgment is the word of grace for his life and salvation. God is never more loving than when he seems most hateful to us. We killed Christ because we wanted to kill God the Enemy in him, who was speaking to us those intolerable words for our healing; and not from that day to this have we quit trying to rid ourselves of him in one way or another.

Before he died, Jesus predicted: "If I be lifted up I will draw all men to myself" (John 12:32). He knew that eventually he would break through the hard crust of our hearts to make the saving change at the center of our being, even though he must die to accomplish it. When he came to us, we saw him as the Enemy and we declared war on him. He might conceivably have said to us: "Very well, have it your way. I come to you in love, to offer you life in place of the death you deserve. But you spurn both giver and gift. I therefore leave you in the sty that you prefer. Wallow in it then, for the rest of time and eternity!" But he did not. He set his face like a flint to go up to Jerusalem. Even as he died he knew that he had not failed. He knew that what we had not heard by the word of his lips we should now, eventually if not immediately, hear by the word of his blood. He knew that he would draw all men to himself, to his Father and theirs. From that day to this he has been doing so, changing us as he draws us into his own image and likeness, reconciling us to God so that for us God the Enemy becomes God the Companion. The "saving Victim" is the saving Victor. To this end was he born; for this purpose came he into the world.

What good did that death of "God on the cross" do to us? To put it quite simply, it reconciled us to him. He had been to us the Void, then the Enemy; but when we respond to the love of God as we see it supremely revealed on Calvary, he becomes to us the Companion: not because he has changed, but because he has changed us toward him.

Thanks be to thee, my Lord Jesus Christ,
For all the benefits thou hast given me,
For all the pains and insults thou hast
    borne for me.
O most merciful Redeemer, Friend, and
    Brother,
May I know thee more clearly,
May I love thee more dearly,
May I follow thee more nearly,
Day by day.

A Twelfth-Century Prayer,
commonly attributed to Richard of Chichester

10

His Dying and Ours

Death is the supreme festival on the road to freedom.

Dietrich Bonhoeffer,
Letters and Papers from Prison

He . . . was crucified, dead, and buried. Of course; nobody
questions that. But why put it into the Creed, as an article of
faith? Historically, the Church had good and sufficient reason for doing so, and for keeping it so. The truth expressed in
these words was questioned and denied by men whose piety
forbade them to believe that the divine Son of God was condemned and killed as a common felon; they found it incredi-
ble that God would ever allow such a thing to happen. Most
of them argued that the event on Calvary was a kind of
shadow-show staged by God to deceive Satan and the human
enemies of God: the real Christ escaped unharmed, while a
phantom resembling him was nailed to the cross. This fantasy
was one of the manifestations of the ancient ultraspirituality
known as gnosticism. It has never died. It is continually bob-
bing up in some usually (but not always) novel form.

Any tendency to minimize the reality of Christ's
suffering—as, for example, by saying that he escaped the
human fear of death by knowing that he would rise again—is
an expression of the gnostic mind. The plain words of the
Creed—suffered, died, was buried, descended into hell—are
meant to exclude anything like that.

Christians have held various beliefs about Christ's descent
into hell. One New Testament writer states that he "went and

preached to the souls in prison" (1 Peter 3:19). It is widely believed that he descended to the realm of the departed to offer his redemption to all who had died before his incarnation. The essential doctrine is that he saves all souls of all ages who humbly receive his gift of eternal life.

But there are two other meanings of the descent into hell. In early English, "hell" and "hole" are from the same root. The grave is a "hell" in the ground. To descend into hell is to become a corpse and be buried. Jesus did this. And he descended into another hell spiritually: the hell in which he cried from his cross, "My God, why have you forsaken me?" It is the hell of feeling forsaken by all who have loved us, even God himself. Jesus descended into this hell by becoming man, for it is a part of the human experience.

The Creed summons us to ponder the way that Jesus died, and Luke speaks of it as his "exodus" which he "accomplished" (Luke 9:31). The words recall the triumphant exodus of the Israelites from their slavery in Egypt under the mighty hand of God. Christ's death was another such victorious pass-over, and any death which is conformed to Christ's death will be such a divine deliverance from bondage to freedom. That explains Bonhoeffer's words, quoted as the text for this chapter, spoken while awaiting death in a Nazi prison. Death is the supreme festival on the road to freedom for any person whose life is "hid with Christ in God" (Colossians 3:3).

Although Jesus died heroically, he did not, as is said of Cawdor in *Macbeth*, throw his life away "as 'twere a careless trifle," and he does not teach us to be nonchalant about our dying. Rousseau said that Socrates died like a philosopher but Christ died like a God. He is clearly right about Socrates; but just how does a God die? I wonder if Rousseau asked himself that question as he coined his epigram. Whatever may be the right way for a God to die, we have the New Testament witness that Jesus agonized in revulsion against the horror of death. He prayed to be spared the ordeal. Whether this is the way Deity dies or not, it is the way man dies when he is entirely human about it. (Perhaps Socrates did not die entirely humanly because his philosophy was not entirely human. Call it suprahuman if you find it splendid and heroic.)

The death on Calvary is the classic death; it became him who tasted death for everyone (Hebrews 2:9) to die as every person dies. Socrates saw death as a divine blessing, since it means the liberation of the divine soul from the prison of the human body. In his last hour he discoursed serenely on the immortality of the soul. Jesus in his last hour cried loudly, wept, and prayed (Hebrews 5:7). He did not welcome death as a kind liberator, and his great interpreter Paul calls death "the last enemy" (1 Corinthians 15:26). To the Hebrew mind, death is an enemy because it separates us from God and therefore from life. Because Jesus' life with God was one of sublime and perfect union, the prospect of death, the total and final separation from God, was uniquely dreadful. Humanly, he was a Hebrew of Hebrews, and he viewed death as such a one. This explains his cry of God-forsakenness as the dread of imminent death possesses him.

Yet, with all his dread, Jesus faced his death faithfully and squarely. He wept not only for himself but for those whom he must leave, and for those who were killing him. He prayed that they might be forgiven. He opened paradise to a man hanging on a nearby cross. Never for a moment, in his worst agony, did he cease to love as he had always loved. And when the final moment came at last, he commended his spirit into the hands of his Father.

From observing the death of the Saving Victor, we may draw several inferences for our own guidance as we face our own death and try to prepare for it. One is that it is not weak, wrong, foolish, or cowardly to dread death or to grieve at the death of others. Jesus wept at the grave of Lazarus. Our dread of death is human, natural, and right; without it we should not value life as we should. This life we have is good, God's precious gift; and if we could part with it without pain or regret, it would be because we hold God's gift in contempt.

But we notice another truth in our Lord's dying which is exemplary for us. Up to the end he does what God has given him to do in this world. He is faithful unto death toward his friends, toward his enemies, and toward those who looked to him for what only he could give them. Nobody who professes to follow Jesus in both his living and dying can fail to learn this lesson well for his own guidance when his time comes. As a parish priest of many years of pastoral experience I have seen many faithful Christians in their acceptance of death and their approach to it, and I have learned from that observation that, when one continues to do his duties and carry his responsibilities up to the very end, or for as long as his strength permits, he dies more calmly and peacefully than would otherwise be the case. When our Lord said, toward his end, "It is finished!" (John 19:30), he expressed that deep peace, even joy, which is given to one who dies in the consciousness that he has done his best to do all that God has given him to do.

Another truth we can learn from Jesus is how to make our death an offering to God of that which he has given us. "No man takes my life from me," said our Lord, "but I am laying it down of my own free will" (John 10:18). The Greek word for "laying it down" implies a willed and purposed action, and we may be sure that it accurately expresses what Jesus said in his own language. He did not want to die, but he did want to offer his life to the Father and he made his death the occasion of this offering. He did not lose his life; he gave it. This self-giving had been his whole life from the beginning: his meat had been to do the will of him who had sent him (John 4:34). And so in his dying he could in his self-giving embrace even the anguish of death. His faith is a paradigm for his followers. Facing our own death, we can include it in our offering of our whole life to the God who gives it. This imitation of Christ gives joy and peace and enhances the value and beauty of life.

Living as we do after both his death and his resurrection, we have something given to us that Jesus himself did not have when he died. We now see his completed conquest of death. We have heard him, returned from the grave, saying to us, "Peace to you!" In the light of his resurrection we see the Last Enemy Death under the control of our mighty Lord, and we know that our dying will be overruled by his love which is stronger than death.

The Roman Catholic Church has wisely canonized Maria Goretti, an Italian child who at the age of eleven was killed by a nineteen-year-old youth while resisting his advances. As she was dying, she said, "God forgive him; I want him in Heaven." She had learned from Jesus how to live and how to die, and in her dying she was more than conqueror through the love of Christ.

We too can learn of him both how to live and how to die.

> My days are few, O fail not,
>   With thine immortal power,
> To hold me that I quail not
>   In death's most fearful hour:
> That I may fight befriended,
>   And see in my last strife
> To me thine arms extended
>   Upon the cross of life.

Paulus Gerhardt, 1656, tr. Robert Bridges, 1899

11

Jesus and Anastasis

Christianity begins where religion ends—with the
Resurrection.

Author unknown

In about A.D. 52 Paul visited the world's most sophisticated
city, Athens. There he preached the gospel to an audience of
people keenly interested in new ideas. It had been rumored
that he was promoting two new Oriental deities named Jesus
and Anastasis (Acts 17:19). *Anastasis* is the Greek word for
resurrection. *Jesus* is the English equivalent of the Greek
effort (*Iesous*) to pronounce the Aramaic name *Yeshua*,
which was the Lord's name in his own tongue.

The Athenians knew nothing about the career of Yeshua, a
Galilean cult leader who had been executed by order of the
Roman governor of the Syrian province, but they had heard
reports that the crucified Yeshua's illegal fraternity was
spreading a wild tale about their leader's resurrection from
the dead. The words *Jesus* and *anastasis* had somehow
become linked. They wondered: Was this new God "Jesus"
before he died, then renamed "Anastasis" after his alleged
resurrection? Or were they two deities? Perhaps their guest
lecturer could set it all straight for them.

Paul told them that Jesus and Anastasis were not two
names for one deity, or two deities, but that Jesus, through
his *anastasis* was the Savior of all people, both Jews and
Greeks. He preached to them Jesus and anastasis—Jesus and
resurrection (Acts 17:18).

The whole gospel is packed into the phrase "Jesus and
anastasis." "Jesus" means "he who saves by the power of

God." The first part of the gospel is that Jesus has this power to save. *Anastasis* means that by a tremendous sign from heaven—his rising from the dead—Jesus is declared to be "the Son of God with power" (Romans 1:4). This second part of the gospel is that Jesus is the ruling King of the universe who delivers his subjects from their bondage to sin and death.

The New Testament records that the risen Lord appears only to "his own"—who believe in him. Theirs is prevenient faith, the faith that precedes vision or demonstration. This is in truth the only real faith. You have faith in somebody *before* he proves by some sign or deed that your faith in him is justified; otherwise, you do not have faith in him. Faith is always a wager, never an I-told-you-so.

Jesus called to himself some ordinary people and asked them to trust and follow him not knowing whither he would lead them. It was before he died and rose again that he said to them, "Believe in me!" It is ever thus. He calls us to follow him before we know him in the power of his resurrection. Even though the historical event of his resurrection has occurred, and we are sure that it happened and that the Lord is risen indeed, for us as for his first followers it is still true that we cannot see our King in the glory of his resurrection except as we trust and obey him to the end of our earthly pilgrimage. Our vision of the King in his beauty is now by faith. It will become sight when we have been raised with him to the life of the world to come.

Christ's resurrection was not a mere survival or a manifestation of the immortality of the soul. He was raised in the flesh. He ate with his friends, let them touch and feel him. His resurrection means the triumph of his whole manhood over death, not just a part of him. Because he is risen in the wholeness of his manhood, he is forever with us as the God-Man. The humanity he received from Mary he has now and forever, as is affirmed in the Athanasian Creed: "He is one not by the transformation of his divinity into flesh, but by the taking up of his humanity into God."

Among the New Testament writers the author of Hebrews has a strong sense of the reality of this "taking up of his humanity into God." He sees the reigning Christ as our eternal high priest who lives forever to intercede for us with the Father, but he sees Christ in heaven not as ex-human but as thoroughly human as ever. "Since he himself has passed through the test of suffering, he is able to help those who are meeting their test now" (2:18). "Ours is not a high priest unable to sympathize with our weaknesses, but one who, because of his likeness to us, has been tested every way" (4:15). He has not forgotten what it is like to be human because he is still and forever human himself.

Modern Christians tend to play down the physical bodiness of the risen Christ: a "purely spiritual" Christ after the resurrection is considered more credible or more appropriate, or both. Clearly, the choice is between believing in a once-dead body raised from a corpse to life and leaving its tomb empty, or believing in what can only be called a spook. (Or perhaps a hallucination? One modernist commentator has said that the disciples' memory of him "quickened into a Presence." If that is what it was, the resurrection as its "witnesses" experienced it was a brainsickly delusion, nothing more.)

It is impossible for dead men to return to life, but with God all things are possible. God did this impossible thing with Jesus to proclaim him "the Son of God with power," so that we may know that the heart that beats upon the throne of the universe is the human heart that wept over Jerusalem and laughed with children.

The body of the risen Christ was his physical body, no less than that; yet there was more than that. The relationship between him and his friends was no longer what it had been before his death. A new aura of transcendence surrounded him. They saw him as now living in both the visible and the invisible worlds. It is beyond our comprehension as it was beyond theirs; but this should not perplex us, for it was an entirely unique phenomenon. When God raised Jesus living from the dead and Jesus appeared to human witnesses, it was an event with no parallel whatever in our history and experience. We are not called upon to understand it, but simply to hear the word which God speaks to us through it. Christ's resurrection is a twofold statement by God to us: a statement about God and a statement about man.

It is first a word about God. He sent his Son into our world in love for us; and, when we killed his Son, he raised him from the dead so that he could continue his rescue mission to us. God's love for us is such that all the hatred for him in hell and on earth cannot change it. The God who raises Jesus from the dead is the God who cannot be discouraged or dissuaded from his purpose to reconcile us to himself.

And it is a word about us. We are the beloved personal objects, the children, of this inexhaustible love. Not only that: we are objects who can be loved into a new state of being which we may call eternal life; we can be raised with Jesus from death to life, not only after the death of our body but in the here and now.

In this world we face two adversaries for which we are no match: sin and death. The power of sin is such that any person in its grip must fail miserably as a person, at every step of his way dragging the chain of all his past sins and adding another link with each new one. Such is our misery outside of Christ, in what we normally call our "natural" condition. In this condition our plight is like that of the chess player whose bad moves bring him at last to that moment of truth when he faces final defeat. A great preacher once used this chess parable. He described the player's hopeless position on the board, then said that the player suddenly shouted, "I see it! I still have another move!" The point of the sermon was that in the game of life a time can come when there is not such another move for the player all on his own, but that there is always another move for the player who knows the living Lord. Christ lives in order to "keep us alive" in this game. In union with him the believer carries on his game, no matter how badly he has fouled himself up with his own bad moves, knowing that Christ provides for him another move. His past moves have altered the course of the game, but he is no longer a slave to his own wretched record because Christ lives to give him forgiveness, grace to amend his life, and light and guidance for the future.

The other great adversary is death. The paths of both glory and shame lead to the grave; therefore, one might reasonably ask what it profits to live for more than the available pleasures and securities of the moment, eating, drinking, and being merry as well as can be managed. A sensible person may thus think about life and its priorities, unless for him Christ is risen. If he is in Christ, he sees another set of possibilities altogether. He sees that the chief end of man is not to cease to exist after life's fitful fever, but to glorify God and to enjoy him forever—beginning here and now. Christ's resurrection proclaims to the mind of faith that he who was dead now lives for us and with us, and that he wills to live in us and through us.

> O God, who for our redemption didst give thine only-begotten Son to the death of the Cross, and by his glorious resurrection hast delivered us from the power of our enemy; Grant us so to die daily from sin, that we may evermore live with him in the joy of his resurrection; through the same thy Son Christ our Lord.
>
> *The Book of Common Prayer*

12

King of the Cosmos

With this ambiguous earth
His dealings have been told us. These abide:
The signal to a maid, the human birth,
The lesson, and the young Man crucified.

But not a star of all
The innumerable hosts of stars has heard
How He administered this terrestrial ball.
Our race have kept their Lord's entrusted Word.

Of His earth-visiting feet
None knows the secret, cherished, perilous,
The terrible, shamefast, frightened, whispered, sweet,
Heart-shattering secret of His way with us.

No planet knows of this.
Our wayside planet, carrying land and wave,
Love and life multiplied, and pain and bliss,
Bears, as chief treasure, one forsaken grave.

Nor, in our little day,
May His devices with the heavens be guessed;
His pilgrimage to thread the Milky Way,
Or His bestowals there, be manifest.

But, in the eternities,
Doubtless we shall gather together, hear
A million alien Gospels, in what guise
He trod the Pleiades, the Lyre, the Bear.

O be prepared, my soul!
To read the inconceivable, to scan
The million forms of God those stars unroll
When, in our turn, we show to them a Man.

Alice Meynell, "Christ in the Universe"

"The Ascension in its simplest terms means that Jesus is
mobile," says Harvey Cox in *The Secular City*. "He is not a

baal, but the Lord of all history." A baal, in the old Semitic theology, was a purely local lord. He had jurisdiction and potency within his territory but not beyond it; he was lord only to his little parcel of land. Christ's ascension is his breaking out from all bounds, even those of space and time, so that he is now lord of all places and all times.

His followers are tempted to try to make a baal of him by making him "one of their own." He has been imaginatively baalized into the Rotarian Jesus, the Aryan Christ, the Black Messiah, and many other shapes and forms. It is a sublime compliment to him that so many want to claim him as their baal. But we cannot possess him; we can only be possessed by him.

The affirmation of Bible and Creed that he ascended into heaven and sits at the right hand of the Father is purposely symbolical; it could not be otherwise, for it refers to an event which begins in time but is consummated in eternity. That event is God's liberation of his Son from his self-imposed limitations of space-time and enthroning him over all the world so that he might be henceforth, in Teilhard's phrase, the shepherd and animator of all creation.

In the first chapter of Acts, Luke describes Christ's ascension in words one would use to describe the flight of a lark toward heaven's gate. He had received his account of the event from eyewitnesses, to whom it had been a visible event. They knew it as a divine miracle to be rejoiced in for its meaning, and they came away from the sight in great joy, knowing that their Lord was now king over all creation. In their minds were such thoughts as these: "I can be in only one place at once, but now Jesus is anywhere and everywhere at once—including wherever I am, in whatever plight I may be." "I live in a body that is easily hurt, easily sickened, and growing old fast. But he who once was vulnerable and mortal like me is no longer so. Yet he will always know what it's like to be this way; he will always carry those wounds."

The heaven to which Christ ascends is the power-center of reality, a "center" which cannot be localized or restricted to any part of the world of being. His session on the right hand of the Father signifies his sharing of world rulership with the Father who does nothing except through the Son.

When Jesus told his sorrowing disciples that it was for their sake that he must go away, they could not see it so. If I do not go, he said, the Holy Spirit cannot come to you (John 16:7ff.). They had to be weaned from total dependence on Christ in his physical presence. The time comes when the good parent or tutor must withdraw from the child in such a way that the child must do more things on his own. No child learns to walk until the stroller is taken from him. Jesus had to withdraw in a certain way—not abandoning his own, but bringing them along in their growth as "sons in the Son."

The prime meaning of the ascension, however, is that there beats upon the throne of the universe the heart which we came to know well when it beat as a human heart in our midst. The strange man who loved us to his own death now rules the world. He can go on giving us that love which lifts and changes us. One symbolic detail of his heavenly enthronement puzzles the modern mind because most of us have had no experience with kings sitting upon thrones. The image evokes in our minds a picture of a medieval monarch, sitting there with nothing to do but to be waited upon and flattered by sycophants. Christ's enthronement means quite the opposite of that—his unceasing triumphant activity. As he "sits," he works, rules, and saves. His sitting is metaphorical, not of repose but of divine power in action.

As "Lord of interstellar space and Conqueror of time" he can be anywhere at any time. A person under sudden temptation may cry, "Jesus, help me!" and his Helper is already there at hand. This same person may have a son in a theater of war on the other side of the planet. He can commend his son to Christ's care knowing that Christ is there with him.

We have seen in our day a substantial revival of interest in "the cosmic Christ." It is a New Testament concept, and the earliest Christians held it strongly. It is the belief that Christ is *in* all the world (not just human souls) as well as *over* it, as its meaning, its shaper, its shepherd, its animator, and its final end. "By him were all things created . . . and by him all things consist" (Colossians 1:16–17). He is "the firstborn of every creature" (Colossians 1:15). He "ascended . . . that he might fill all things" (Ephesians 4:10). Christ rules not only the souls of his saints but all things that exist, animate and inanimate, visible and invisible.

The great reviver of this vision of Christ has been Teilhard de Chardin. Oddly, almost nowhere in his writings does he refer specifically to the ascension of Christ; he simply assumes this transition from Christ in the flesh to Christ the glorified Lord of all. But he dwells constantly upon the activity of Christ in the world as its shepherd and animator. Paul declares that Christ "must reign till he has put all enemies under his feet" (1 Corinthians 15:25), meaning that Christ must finish his work of "christifying" (Teilhard's term) all that is not yet subject to his loving rule.

Teilhard writes in *Hymn of the Universe*: "Since Jesus was born, and grew to his full stature, and died, everything has continued to move forward *because Christ is not yet fully formed*: he has not yet gathered about him the last folds of his robe of flesh and of love which is made up of his faithful followers. The mystical Christ has not yet attained to his full growth; and therefore the same is true of the cosmic Christ. Both of these are simultaneously in the state of being and of becoming; and it is from the prolongation of this process of becoming that all created activity ultimately springs. Christ is the end point of the evolution, even the *natural* evolution, of all beings; and therefore evolution is holy" (p. 133).

While on the battlefront of the First World War Teilhard

was working out his basic beliefs, and in doing so he was pulled by two forces: one, the movement of human development; the other, the upward and Godward movement of Christian worship. He came to see Christ as the God "ahead" and the God "on high." The meeting and merging of these two movements—the first, evolution; the second, redemption—is what he calls the "christification" of the universe.

One need not be a complete Teilhardian to see the cosmic Christ as redeemer, animator, "christifier" of the whole creation, who works primarily through human agents. It is an important and heartening fact that responsible people today are growing sensitive in conscience about such things as water pollution and other antinatural results of man's irresponsible behavior. This conscience, belatedly born, is the work of Christ the shepherd and animator "by whom all things consist." This is an important facet of the ascension mystery of Christ which we are rediscovering in our day. Man shows his own christification by working with his Lord in the christification of the whole world of people, other living creatures, and things.

The Collect for the Ascension with which we shall close this chapter recalls Christ's ascending into heaven and prays that his faithful ones "may also in heart and mind thither ascend, and with him continually dwell." Christ can lift his people into that dimension of life which we call heaven—here and now. He calls them to renounce this world's way of thinking and living and to rise to his way of thinking and living, and that is to ascend into heaven, for heaven is wherever God's will is done and his creatures rejoice in his goodness and beauty. There is an old story about an English soldier in the Crimean War who was lying wounded in a field hospital. He had been delirious for days when Florence Nightingale stopped by his bed. Suddenly he awoke to full consciousness and asked, "Is this heaven?" Heaven had entered his ward, stood by his bed, and touched him, through one who had ascended with Christ.

> Grant, we beseech thee, Almighty God, that like as we do believe thy only-begotten Son our Lord Jesus Christ to have ascended into the heavens; so we may also in heart and mind thither ascend, and with him continually dwell, who liveth and reigneth with thee and the Holy Ghost, one God, world without end.
>
> *The Book of Common Prayer*

13

Marana tha!

Only our concept of time makes it possible for us to speak of the Day of Judgment by that name; in reality it is a summary court in perpetual session.

Franz Kafka

As the new faith spread out into the gentile world, it embraced people whose language was not Hebrew or Aramaic but Greek. The gospel had to be translated into their language. Some Hebrew or Aramaic expressions, such as *Abba, Amen,* and *Alleluia,* were carried over bodily without translation. Among these Aramaic phrases was *Marana tha!* It became a watchword of early Christianity.

Marana tha can be either a petition looking toward a future fulfillment—"Our Lord, come!"—or an assertion of past and present fact—"Our Lord has come!" It meant both of these to the first Christians. They were vividly aware that Christ had come in great humility, in the flesh. They were vividly aware that he was with them now, invisibly but invincibly. And they were vividly aware that he would come again in glorious majesty at the end of this age to judge the living and the dead and to establish his everlasting kingdom. They lived in both hope and fulfillment, and *Marana tha!* expressed the longing of the hope and the joy of the fulfillment. They saw themselves as the interim people whose calling was to occupy, to hold the line, until his coming again. They watched and waited for the Lord to come, but they were not idle as they did so. They laid their lives on the line witnessing for him, professing him before all peoples, and suffering much for his sake.

What made their lot endurable and even joyful was their conviction that Christ would come soon, any day, any moment, and that he would wipe away all tears and inaugurate his reign over all the earth. Thus their very life was expressed in *Marana tha!*

As the years of waiting stretched into decades, then centuries, this joyful anticipation of Christ's coming again gradually changed from eager joy to boding fear. The Last Day became the dreaded Judgment Day which filled Christian hearts with terror. The doctrine of the Second Coming became a grim warning of divine retribution, replacing the original bright promise of the final victory of Christ's faithful people with their Lord. Modern Christians have revolted against this doctrinal corruption, but many have forgotten that the corruption of a truth does not abolish the truth itself. It is an essential article of the Christian faith that Christ will come with glory to judge the living and the dead.

To think at all helpfully about Christ as judge, we must rid our minds of all associations with courtrooms, benches, juridical verdicts and sentences, for these are badly misleading. A human judge on the bench is there to vindicate and execute the law of man. The judge may be a good man himself, but the defendant is not judged by his success or failure in measuring up to the judge's personal rectitude. The defendant is judged by the written law of his society rather than by the character of the judge. Christ's judgment is entirely different. Under it we are judged not by any law but by Christ himself. Are we conformed to him in our own being? That is the only criterion.

Christ's judging is already taking place, and we are undergoing it whether we are aware of it or not. It has been going on ever since his first coming. His judgment is remedial, not retributive. He invites all to come to him, and coming to him means coming under the silent judgment of his presence. In him we see our own selves as we are meant to be, and this contrast between the person who is and the person whom God intends is a judgment that shatters our self-satisfaction, once we are given to see it.

It is often remarked that, when we see a Rembrandt painting or hear a Beethoven symphony, we cannot judge it—we can only respond to it. Our response to it is its judgment upon us. Likewise, our response to Christ is a judgment upon us. Teilhard's conception of this, as presented in *The Divine Milieu*, is illuminating: "The Kingdom of God is within us. When Christ appears in the clouds He will simply be manifesting a metamorphosis that has been slowly accomplished under His influence in the heart of the mass of mankind. In order to hasten His coming, let us therefore concentrate upon a better understanding of the process by which the Holy Presence is born and grows within us" (pp. 107–8).

There will come a moment of final wrap-up of all human history. (I call it a moment, and this term normally means a point in time. If there was a temporal moment when human history began, there must be a temporal moment when it will end. But if anybody wants to place that "moment" in eternity, I shall not argue.) In that final wrap-up every life, every institution, will be judged by one test: its fitness for Christ's kingdom. This is what Christians ought to mean by the Last Judgment. To believe that the Christ who once came among us is King of the Cosmos is to believe that the whole world, everybody and everything, stands or falls by this test of conformity to him. To believe in his first coming as Savior is to believe in his final coming as Judge.

Essential though this belief is, however, it is futuristic, and Christ wants his followers to live in the present; indeed, their present determines their future. In countless ways he drives this truth home to us in his parables and pronouncements.

He told the story of the rich fool who built one barn after another to contain his ever-growing wealth. Then one night the Lord said to him, "You fool! Your life is now required of you, and what becomes of all this stuff you've been piling up?" The man was a fool because he lived for the false and problematical riches of the future rather than for the true and certain riches available to him in the present: love of God and love of neighbor.

The reader of the Gospels is struck by Christ's constant insistence upon the unexpectedness of the moment of judgment. The Judge comes suddenly like a thief in the night.

In the most dramatic parable of judgment (Matthew 25:31–46) all are judged solely on the basis of what they did to Christ mystically present in "the least" of human beings here and now in the flesh.

In several parables and pronouncements Jesus teaches us to think of our Master as absent for a time and of ourselves as his servants occupying ourselves until he comes. In an experience of many years ago I learned something about Christ's coming in judgment. At the age of eighteen I aspired to be a journalist. The editor of a rural weekly newspaper gave me my first job. The Great Depression gripped the land, and he could not really afford to hire me even for the little that he paid; but he was interested in me and my future and wanted to help me get started. One day he left on a trip, telling us that he would be gone for two weeks. Instantly I and the other employees slacked off. Our thought was that a day or so before his return we would get to work and tidy things up and pretend that we had been hammering away like Titans. But he came back earlier than he had planned. He walked straight into the midst of our slovenly mess. I remember a paleness and a pain on his face, but he said nothing then. The next morning he called us all together. He told us how much the paper's income had fallen off in recent months. He said that he hoped he could keep it alive and that he wouldn't have to let any of us go, because it would be impossible for us to get jobs anywhere else. That was all. I can testify that ever since then I have had some conscience about betraying the trust of those who trust me as that man Riley Morgan (God rest and refresh his soul) trusted me, as the Lord trusts us all.

One further note about that incident: Mr. Morgan did not condemn us. We condemned ourselves. I stood self-condemned by my failure to keep faith with him who had shown faith in me. That is the nature of our experience of Christ's judgment, which is remedial and healing rather than vindictive and punitive. For that reason the Christian should accept Christ's judgment not with cringing servile fear but with the filial fear which Francis J. Hall defines as "loving anxiety to please God."

Although Christ is not a "hanging judge" and his judgment is for healing, it may well make painful demands upon the judged because it works purgation of the evil. But the evil is purged so that the good can replace it, and we should keep our eye upon this benefit. We may have this benefit of his judgment now, if we seek it and welcome it. Now, in the time of this mortal life, the sinful soul can cast off the works of darkness and put on the armor of light, thus preparing responsibly for the final accounting.

"The end of all things is at hand" (1 Peter 4:7). This was another watchword of the early Christians. They did not find it a frightening prospect, but a hope that gave rich and glad meaning to their troubled existence. The end of all things is at hand; therefore rejoice! That end is not the dead end but the living end, the end that has already appeared in the person of Jesus. The End had been with them in the flesh, and men like Peter and John had eaten with him, walked with him, laughed, joked, worked, and wept with him. Then he, the End of all things, had been murdered by his enemies. Then he had been raised living from the dead and exalted by God's power to the throne of the universe. Not only was he high and lifted up over all creation, he was most intimately at hand, closer than breathing, nearer than hands and feet, with them as indwelling Lord, Friend, Companion, and Savior. He asked them to wait patiently for a while, suffering the worst the world could do to them. Then would come the End in final victory, peace, and joyous life in his kingdom and presence forever.

Such was the belief of the first Christians, and it is the right expectation for Christians of any age. We need not be put off by the fact that they were evidently mistaken about the time factor. They expected the End to come within their lifetime, and it did not. Their error was only a bad guess about what God would do next, and exactly how and when he would do it. Evidently they had forgotten their Master's plain warning that no man can know the hour of his coming (Mark 13:32). A thousand years in God's sight are as a watch in the night.

We know all that we need to know. He who is the End, to whom all nations shall bow, has already appeared. We have seen the End, and we belong to him. We know what he asks of us while we await his coming, for we know him as he is. *Marana tha!*

> Almighty God, give us grace that we may cast away the works of darkness, and put upon us the armour of light, now in the time of this mortal life, in which thy Son Jesus Christ came to visit us in great humility; that in the last day, when he shall come again in his glorious majesty to judge both the quick and the dead, we may rise to the life immortal, through him who liveth and reigneth with thee and the Holy Ghost, now and ever.
>
> *The Book of Common Prayer*

14

The Lord-Spirit

Those who have the gale of the Holy Spirit go forward even in sleep.

Brother Lawrence

Three centuries ago Sir Thomas Browne, a devout physician, wrote in his *Religio Medici:* "I am sure there is a common Spirit that plays within us, yet makes no part of us; and that is the Spirit of God, the fire and scintillation of that noble and mighty Essence which is the life and radical heat of spirits and those essences that know not the virtue of the sun: a fire quite contrary to the fire of Hell. This is that gentle heat that brooded on the waters, and in six days hatched the world; this is the irradiation that dispels the mists of Hell, the clouds of horror, fear, sorrow, despair, and preserves the region of the mind in serenity. Whosoever feels not the warm gale and gentle ventilation of this Spirit, though I feel his pulse I dare not say he lives: for truly, without this, to me there is no heat under the Tropic, nor any light, though I dwelt in the body of the Sun."

Sir Thomas's language is not the language of today, but we understand him. There is in all men "a common Spirit" which works in us but is not a part of our natural being. It is warm, even fiery, but not like the fire of hell: a creative fire, not destructive. It is this Spirit which brooded over the primeval waters, bringing order from chaos. As this Spirit rules in our lives, his brightness scatters all clouds of fear, sadness, and despair. We truly live only as this Spirit lives in us.

The familiar English text of the Nicene Creed calls this Spirit "the Lord, and Giver of life." In the original Greek text, there is a sense that does not come through in English. It speaks of him as the Lord-Spirit (*to Pneuma to hagion*) and Maker-alive (*to zōopoion*). This reflects the New Testament understanding of the Spirit. Bible and Creed assume that there are two necessary dimensions of human life. We can have animal life and be physically as healthy and exuberant as a colt; but if there is not something else in us that sets us apart from healthy animals, it must be said that, for all our energy, we are not truly alive. A person is alive only when he has mind and spirit, is able to think, plan, judge, make choices—and mistakes, and cooperate consciously with God in his work of creation.

C. S. Lewis makes clear the distinction in this way in *Mere Christianity*: "In reality, the difference between Biological life and Spiritual life is so important that I am going to give them two distinct names. The Biological sort which comes to us through Nature, and which (like everything else in Nature) is always tending to run down and decay so that it can only be kept up by incessant subsidies from Nature in the form of air, water, food, etc., is *Bios*. The Spiritual life which is in God from all eternity, and which made the whole natural universe, is *Zoe*. *Bios* has, to be sure, a certain shadowy or symbolic resemblance to *Zoe*: but only the sort of resemblance there is between a photo and a place, or a statue and a man. A man who changed from having *Bios* to having *Zoe* would have gone through as big a change as a statue which changed from being a carved stone to being a real man.

"And that is precisely what Christianity is about. This world is a great sculptor's shop. We are the statues and there is a rumour going around the shop that some of us are some day going to come to life" (book IV, chap. 1).

Jesus told an inquiring intellectual named Nicodemus that, unless a man is born again of the Spirit, he cannot enter the kingdom of God (John 3:5), which is a way of saying that a man cannot come alive without this birth from *Bios* to *Zoe*.

Before this birth, a man is the statue or scale-model of a man; the Spirit turns him from pre-man into man. The Spirit regenerates us from *Bios* to *Zoe*, then nurtures and guides our growth in *Zoe*—the life that we see perfectly manifested in Christ.

The Lord-Spirit is, however, the giver of life in all stages, not just of *Zoe*. When a fetus is conceived, it is the work of the Spirit. All *Bios* is his gift; every living creature is conceived by his agency. This being so, it may seem to be doubtfully wise to talk about two kinds of life, biological and spiritual, since all life is ultimately one. But life is vertically and hierarchically organized, not horizontally and all on a level. The earthworm and the angel, the sperm cell and the sage of ninety years, share a common life, but they are not alive in the same ways and on the same level. Nor are all people alive in the same ways and on the same level. We are all of us *more or less* alive, and the Holy Spirit wants to make us more alive. A prayer in a fourth-century liturgy reads: "We beseech thee, make us living men." Only one man who ever lived was fully alive. As the Spirit shows us our own glorious potentialities in Christ, we can only beseech him to make us alive as Christ is alive.

A Voice within us keeps whispering, "Grow! You must grow, and you can. Trust Me. Draw upon Me. I am Growth. I am Life. Let Me give you growth and life." This is the voice of the Lord-Spirit, the Maker-alive.

Zealous Christians, meaning well but not thinking well, have seldom made a worse mistake than when they have attacked "evolution" as an enemy to faith in God as the Creator. To be sure, the evolutionary theory of the origin and development of man is only a theory, and it may not be true. I am saying only that they are wrong who say that, if evolution is true, belief in divine creation must be false, and vice versa. Anyone who truly believes in the Maker-alive to whom the Bible testifies should have no difficulty believing that, if life evolves from lower to higher, it is the work of the Lord-Spirit who gives growth, development, upward mobility. This is well expressed in the familiar poem "Each in His Own Tongue" by William Herbert Carruth:

> A fire-mist and a planet—
>   A crystal and a cell,
> A jelly-fish and a saurian,
>   And caves where the cave-men dwell;
> Then a sense of law and beauty
>   And a face turned from the clod,—
> Some call it Evolution,
>   And others call it God.

So runs the first stanza. What the poet calls Consecration in the last stanza is a fruit of the same Spirit:

> A picket frozen on duty,
>   A mother starved for her brood,
> Socrates drinking the hemlock,
>   And Jesus on the rood;
> And millions who, humble and nameless,
>   The straight, hard pathway plod,—
> Some call it Consecration,
>   And others call it God.

How can we know if we are in the Spirit, and growing in him? About this we never need to be in the dark: Christ is the criterion. If the Spirit is doing his work with us, we are growing up into Christ (Ephesians 4:15); we are conscious of an increase within ourselves of the fruits of the Spirit—"love, joy, peace, patience, kindness, goodness, fidelity, gentleness, and self-control" (Galatians 5:22). To this list of fruits of the Spirit may be added sensitivity, or sensibility. In *Heretics*, G. K. Chesterton wrote: "When Nietzsche says, 'A new commandment I give to you, *Be hard*,' he is really saying, 'A new commandment I give to you, *Be dead.'* Sensibility is the definition of life."

The Spirit of God fills the whole world. We know and experience him most immediately as God carrying on his creation of the world through us. He is the life and power of the Church: eminently ecclesiastical, but not exclusively so. He is more catholic even than the Catholic Church. He sponsors and executes every good thought, word, or deed ever thought, spoken, or done by angel or man. His field is the universe, and no living creature lies beyond the range of his creative fire divine.

Eternal Love, maintain thy life in me!

Sir Philip Sidney

15

The Church

The Church of Christ is not an institution; it is a
new life with Christ and in Christ, guided by the
Holy Spirit.

Sergius Bulgakov, *The Orthodox Church*

In Jude (verse 3) an early Christian writer speaks of "the common salvation." It is his description of Christianity. He means that there is no private salvation, and all the New Testament writers agree with him. To be in Christ is to belong to a family and to share with the other members "the common salvation." Salvation is the state of being whole, complete persons in the likeness of Christ. It is not so much a matter of where we are going when we die as of who and what we are becoming while we live. We are completely saved when we are completely conformed to Christ. Salvation is an eminently *personal* matter but not at all a private matter; it is a family matter. For as soon as we respond lovingly to the love of God in Christ, he introduces us to our brothers and sisters in his family, with whom we share the common salvation. If we lack this loving awareness of those others, our response to Christ has not been one of love, for we cannot love him and ignore those others for whom he died.

The gentle John says bluntly: "If a man says 'I love God' while he hates his brother he is a liar; for he who loves not his brother whom he has seen, how can he love God whom he has not seen?" (1 John 4:20). Of course, this way of putting it raises a question. May not the fact that we *have* seen our brother, and know him "only too well," make it harder for us to love him? It is easier to love the Chinese peasant whom we have not seen than the neighbor who poisoned our dog. I'm sure John would agree with us about this and would say that we grow in love, hence as human beings sharing the common salvation, only as we strive with all our hearts to love the not easily lovable.

It is my conviction, born of more than forty years' experience in the ministry, that God gives us "difficult" brothers and sisters in the Church precisely for the purpose of giving us this arduous exercise in loving the not easily lovable, because without this we cannot grow in grace and Christlikeness. It is the Lord's doing. He gives us these hard-to-love brothers and sisters and commands us to love them as part of the divine regimen which has our salvation as its end and goal. The bores, scoundrels, and hypocrites in the Church are as necessary to our salvation as faith and the divinely appointed sacraments.

What I have said is, I realize, flatly counter to a very familiar attitude which says: "I would gladly belong to the Church if the people in it were all that they ought to be as Christians—saints whose very sitting next to me would make me a better person. But as it is, the people I see in the Church are mostly no better than I am, and some of them not even so good; so what would I gain by joining them?"

If this person's assessment is correct, he needs to be in the Church if for no other reason than to learn to love those whom he now despises.

In *The Book of Common Prayer* the Church is defined as "the Body of which Jesus Christ is the Head, and all baptized people are the members." Probably ninety-five percent of all Christians would accept this. The common salvation is the sharing of the divine life which flows from the Head through the body. We are given the knowledge and love of God, we are conformed to Christ, we are saved, as we lovingly participate in this sharing. We all realize, when we think about it, that man is a social animal; hence, there can be no completeness of being for him in solitude or in isolation from others. The Church is necessary to our completeness because of our social nature as well as because of the divine life that is shared within its fellowship.

So then, the exercise of loving our hard-to-love brethren is part of God's saving treatment. If we would love him, we must love them. The Church is, among other things, a gymnasium in which we develop the sinews of the soul by that exercise along with other disciplines. But it is not only, or primarily, this. The Church is the home—headquarters, if you will—of the Holy Spirit upon earth, and in it are the means of grace which the Lord especially provides for the spiritual nurture of his people. This is not to say that there are no means of grace outside the Church. It is to say that God provides certain means and devices for our growth in the knowledge and love of himself, and he has committed these to his Church.

When those of the Church speak of the means of grace, they often mean the Sacraments in particular, and these are indeed means by which God gives to hungry souls the manna of his love. But there are other means of grace within the Church. We have already spoken of the paradoxical but very real one—the work of learning to love the unlovable in Christ. Then there is worship apart from the Sacraments. There is the Bible as a written means of grace, and it is the Church's book, not the world's. There is the fellowship of kindred and congenial minds as well as the uncongenial, for in the Church we meet not only the hard to love and the impossible to admire, we meet also those who are in every way better than we are, in whose fellowship we cannot but grow. There is the Church's service of a needy world. All of these are means of grace, which means opportunities for growth. Any soul can profit from them as he finds them in any congregation of Christians—unless he is too proud to accept their help.

It must be recognized, however, that some of us have a strong taste for the Church, while others who hunger and thirst for the living God have a strong distaste for it. Some reject the Church out of mere snobbery and egotism, thinking that they are too good for it. But others stand outside the Church for less discreditable reasons. Among these are people who know that the Church as a historical institution has something of a "past" in the uncomplimentary sense. In countless times and ways it has seemed to betray its Master by the sins of its leaders and its people. But whoever appeals to history must appeal to the whole of history. There is not only the dark mystery of iniquity in the Church's scoundrels, there is also the bright mystery of sanctity in the Church's saints; and be it well noted that outside the Church there are no saints.

I have just made an astounding statement, now that I look back over it—perhaps an outrageous one. But I know of no saints outside the Church; I have never met one, never even heard of one. There have always been wonderful people of great goodness outside the Church. They, too, are God's human handiwork, and God is to be praised and thanked for them. They live by their own resources of character; and since God gave them both their character and their resources, he is the ultimate sole source of their goodness. But consciously and in their own mind they achieve their own goodness. The saint is no such achiever. He is the purely dependent and derivative person who says—and means—"I can of myself do nothing. I can do all things through Christ who is my strength, my life, and my salvation." Paul Tillich noted that the saint is saint not because he is "good," but because he is transparent for something beyond himself. That something is Christ, the divine Somebody.

The Church's mission to its own members is to make saints of them. How well it has really done its work over the past nearly two thousand years only God knows, because the number and identity of the saints are known only to him.

Others are troubled not so much by the Church's past scandals as by its present stodginess and dullness. They think that the knowledge, love, worship, and service of God must be always exciting and thrilling, and they do not always find the Church so. They feel let down by the cheap art, the drab architecture, the pedestrian preaching, the syrupy music, and the bourgeois membership. People instinctively look for the best in brains, art, and music as well as spirituality when they enter the Church. If they do not find it there, it is the fault, or at least the inadequacy, of those who are in the Church. But these God-seekers who are turned off by the mediocrity of the people on the inside need to be told, as lovingly and yet as plainly as possible, that they need to be cured of their pride before they can enter. They are no better than those inside. He who wants communion with God outside the Church is seeking salvation on his own terms rather than God's terms. God calls nobody to become a hidebound ecclesiastic; he calls everybody to take his place in the family life of those who are God's family.

Another difficulty which trips up some is intellectual difficulty with some church doctrines and practices. About this it needs to be said without any equivocation or apology that the great Christian truths cannot be apprehended by the mind alone, but only by the mind in loving partnership with the heart. Goethe rightly declared: "Man can understand nothing except as he loves it." To test this rule, we may apply it to the Christian dogma which seems to give the most intellectual offense to the most people—the Holy Trinity. The dogma is preposterous to the mind that sees it only as a propositional description of the Godhead. But the Christian belief that God is one God in three Persons comes out of—and is sustained by—the Christian experience of loving God and being loved by God. Knowing that the Father's love creates us, the Son's love recalls us to God and redeems us, and the Holy Spirit's love strengthens and sanctifies us, we lovingly respond in the only way possible, by adoring the Triune Love.

The love of God is the ground, the source, the shaper, and the sustainer of all the Christian dogmas, and the God-seeker may be sure that, if he will approach these holy mysteries using love rather than logic as his key, the door to understanding will be opened to him. The Lord of the Church does not command his faithful to understand all mysteries in this present life. Now we know in part. He says to them: As I have loved you, so you ought to love one another (John 13:34). If we enter his Church in humble, hungry, loving response to his invitation, in his light we begin to see light, and as we continue in this holy fellowship the light will grow.

> O God, of unchangeable power and eternal light, look favorably on thy whole Church, that wonderful and sacred mystery; and, by the tranquil operation of the perpetual Providence, carry out the work of man's salvation; and let the whole world feel and see that things which were cast down are being built up, and things which had grown old are being made new; through Jesus Christ thy Son our Lord.
>
> Author unknown

16

The Communion of Saints

They that love beyond the world cannot be separated by it. Death is but a crossing the world, as friends do the seas; they live in one another still.

William Penn

Some years ago I was visiting an old country church in South Carolina. In the churchyard I stopped to read the names and dates on one family plot. They told the story of the mother of six children who died more than a century ago after bearing these children—all of whom died in infancy or early childhood. Instantly I found myself praying: "Dear God, You hold all souls in life, and these are Your children. Give them joy and life in Your bright presence forever!" The prayer was not a pious act of mine. Indeed, because it was a true prayer it was not mine at all, but God's: the Holy Spirit praying through me. In that moment I was participating in the communion of saints. "Communion" is a verbal noun. It isn't merely something we belong to, it is something we do: or, more accurately, something that God does through us.

Not long after that, I read in Jim Bishop's newspaper column an account of his friendship with the Kennedy family. He recalled a visit to the elder Kennedys at their Florida home, at a time after both John and Robert had been assassinated. Old Mr. Kennedy, now an invalid, began to weep helplessly. Then Rose Kennedy said, "Let me show you something." She led him to a window, pointed to a swimming pool, and here I quote Mr. Bishop: " 'They all grew up there,' she said softly. Rose smiled. She saw it peopled with splashing, shouting children." She smiled rather than wept because she saw those children not in the "dear dead days beyond recall" but in the eternal present. Bishop went on to report that after John's death Rose Kennedy sometimes shattered her friends by calmly remarking, "I mean to speak to the President about that when I see him." She was living in the communion of saints. Like every other article of the Christian Creed, the communion of saints is rooted and grounded in the experience of loving God, and being loved by God, in Christ.

As an article of faith it is based upon two things: first, God's showing himself to us in Christ as our Father, whence we understand that, if we are God's children, we are all one beloved and eternal family; and second, our experience of loving and being loved within that family. What was it that moved me at that graveside to pray for those people who had died long before I was born? Why did they mean anything to me? Why did I suppose that I could possibly do anything to assuage their affliction, suffered while they were here in the flesh? I am not a compassionate man beyond the ordinary. It could only be because the Spirit moved me to reach out to these, my living brothers and sisters in the family of our common Father. I wanted to send out to them my love and care through the universe. Only God could convey the message from my heart to them, and I am sure that he did—and eternally does. I am equally sure that they respond with their blessing upon me, which, again, only God can convey. I am their brother upon earth. They are my brothers and sisters in heaven. They are more lovingly aware of me than I can be of them because, living as they do in God's Nearer Presence, they enjoy powers of loving and helping far beyond mine; but they and I are mutually loving, helping, caring for one another in the communion of saints. (When we use the word "saints" in this connection, we mean simply all who live in Christ and are being sanctified by the Spirit.)

We grow in our awareness of this living and indestructible family of all who live in Christ by fixing our minds upon all the love we have received from those who have gone before us and who now—in ways unknown to us—continue to help us by their love. Our immediate benefactors such as our parents and others whom we have known directly come most readily to mind. Our debt to them is obvious, though incalculable. But I may also believe, and in fact I do, that a thousand years ago there lived somebody (and the name is legion) who at that time was doing things that benefit me a thousand years later. I don't know who that person was and is, but God knows. I don't know what that person did on earth that helps me so much now or what that person is doing now in that Larger Life that helps me now and will help me forever, but God knows, and through his Spirit assures me that it is so. This benefactor whose name is legion is unknown to me but well-known to God. Is there any way that I can help my benefactor? I can think of at least two ways. First, I can strive to be the kind of person upon whom his help has not been wasted. We are surrounded by a great cloud of witnesses (Hebrews 12:1) who are our benefactors, and we can rejoice their hearts by doing our best as faithful servants of their Lord and ours. Second, we can pray for them. Interceding for those departed this life should present no theological problem for us if we bear in mind that, when we pray for anybody, whether in the flesh or out of it, we simply commend that person to God's love and care. We are more than content to leave it to God to decide how he will answer it, and we rejoice that it is so because we know that he is doing for that person better things than we can desire or pray for.

I have hesitated to put into this book what I am about to say, not because I am of doubtful mind about its truth but because I've never read it or heard anybody else say it (which doesn't mean, of course, that nobody else has ever thought of it). With me it is a private opinion, but I don't mind making it public. It is a belief prompted and sponsored in me by the closing verse of one of my favorite chapters in the Bible: Hebrews 11, well called "the Westminster Abbey of the

Bible" because there the heroes and heroines of God's people are immortally honored. The author concludes his roll call of the elect by saying in effect that, although these mighty saints died in faith and are now glorified, apart from you and me they will not "be made perfect." God will complete them *through us*. All who have gone before us and have striven to serve God faithfully await a fulfillment which we can make possible for them by being faithful in our own day. It is natural, and right, for Christians to think about the good things that those who have gone ahead of us can do for us. I believe it is *equally* in order for us to think about what we can do for them that will contribute to their eternal and triumphant completion.

This should not strike us as a strange or novel concept if we understand with Paul that God has made us all members one of another. The communion of saints is our mutual membership in Christ *sub specie aeternitatis*—in its eternal dimension. All of your ancestors and benefactors of times past, and you, and all of your biological and spiritual descendants through ages yet to come, are mutually dependent upon one another for your and their perfection, completion, and fulfillment. They without you cannot be made perfect; you without them cannot be made perfect. I find it a thought sometimes inspiring and sometimes sobering, even frightening—depending upon how I'm doing with my own life at the moment.

> O almighty God, who hast knit together thine elect in one communion and fellowship, in the mystical body of thy Son Christ our Lord; Grant us grace so to follow thy blessed Saints in all virtuous and godly living, that we may come to those unspeakable joys which thou hast prepared for those who unfeignedly love thee; through the same thy Son Jesus Christ our Lord.
>
> *The Book of Common Prayer*

17

The Forgiveness of Sins

The forgiveness of God is the foundation of every
bridge from a hopeless past to a courageous
present.

George Adam Smith

The forgiveness of sins is placed in that final section of the
Creed which speaks of the Holy Spirit, the Church, the Communion of Saints, the Resurrection of the body, and the Life
everlasting. There is a reason for this. The forgiveness of sins
belongs to that new life which is given to us when the Holy
Spirit takes us over, to re-create us into the likeness of Christ.

We begin our eternal life when we are baptized into
Christ's body, the Church, and are made participants in the
communion of saints. God then gets us started growing and
developing into the divine likeness. But our growing up in
Christ does not follow a swift, smooth, and easy course. It is
hard, slow, often painful, because we keep on sinning, and
our sins stunt us, block us, and sidetrack us. If we are not to
abandon our effort in despair, we must believe in the forgiveness of our sins as we try to make our way forward toward
our goal in Christ.

We cannot get on with our growing unless God gives us a
fresh start whenever we need it, and that is at every turn of
our way. Forgiveness means just that: a fresh start. Without
it we are bound and shackled by what we have done and
what we have been. The difficulty that many people find in
believing in the forgiveness of sins comes from their observation, which is entirely correct, that what's done is done and
can never be undone. If forgiveness consisted of the undoing

of what is done, they would be right; but it is not. When God forgives us, he accepts us as we are, however soiled we may be, and he says, "Let's get on from here. My grace is made perfect in your weakness. Trust me more, yourself less."

There is a peculiar feature of the Christian understanding of God's forgiveness, and that is the teaching of Jesus that God will forgive us only as we forgive others. "When you stand praying, forgive, if you have a grievance against anybody, so that your Father in heaven can forgive your trespasses" (Mark 11:25). As a Christian I accept that this is so because he who is the Word and Wisdom of God Incarnate assures us that it is. But it is easier, for me and for many others, to accept it theologically than to apply it to cases in life. Our difficulty is not in receiving forgiveness from God but in giving forgiveness to other people. Here is a statement from Bertrand Russell, the eminent English philosopher, written in 1945:

"Let us think of some of the things that are likely to happen in our time to inhabitants of Europe or China. Suppose you are a Jew, and your family has been massacred. Suppose you are an underground worker against the Nazis, and your wife has been shot because you could not be caught. Suppose your husband, for some purely imaginary crime, has been sent to forced labor in the Arctic, and has died of cruelty and starvation. Suppose your daughter has been raped and then killed by enemy soldiers. Ought you, in these circumstances, to preserve a philosophic calm?

"If you follow Christ's teaching, you will say 'Father, forgive them, for they know not what they do.' I have known Quakers who could have said this sincerely and profoundly, and whom I admired because they could. But before giving admiration one must be very sure that the misfortune is felt as deeply as it should be. One cannot accept the attitude of some among the Stoics, who said, 'What does it matter to me if my family suffer? I can still be virtuous.' The Christian principle, 'Love your enemies,' is good, but the Stoic princi- ple, 'Be indifferent to your friends,' is bad. And the Christian principle does not inculcate calm, but an ardent love towards the worst of men. There is nothing to be said against it except that it is too difficult for most of us to practice sincerely."

There is nothing in the foregoing statement from *A History of Western Philosophy* (p. 578) with which any thoughtful Christians cannot agree. The free, unconditional, loving for- giveness of all who wrong us is indeed most difficult for us to practice, and the best of Christians must rely wholly upon God's grace to enable him to do it. It is terribly easy to deceive ourselves about this by imagining that we have for- given somebody—sufficiently at least—when we have not done so at all. There is an instructive example of this in Jane Austen's *Pride and Prejudice*. Mr. Collins, a pompous young clergyman, is counseling somebody who has been wronged by several people, and he says: "You ought certainly to for- give them, as a Christian, but never to admit them in your sight, or allow their names to be mentioned in your hearing." When you forgive somebody, you embrace him with your heart and you love him as if the wrong had not been done. Anything less or other than that is not forgiveness.

Our Christian belief in forgiveness has two fronts, one fac- ing toward God and the other toward man. We look to God for his forgiveness of our sins, and we look to our fellowmen to forgive them their wrongs against us and to hope for their forgiveness of us, for we must always be mindful that we need not only God's forgiveness but man's. We have sinned, in thought, word, and deed, against God and against our neighbor at every turn of our way.

That God forgives us is the great good news of the gospel. We are forgiven through Jesus Christ: that is to say, Christ brings to us the forgiveness of God. "He died that we might be forgiv'n, he died to make us good." Why, then, did so staunch a Christian as Martin Luther make the following statement? "Forgiveness of sins ought to make you rejoice; that is the very heart of Christianity, and yet it is a mighty dangerous thing to preach." He meant that we shall be tempted to grow presumptuous as we think of God's free pardon, so that we say, "How wonderfully good of God! That takes care of my sins: God forgives me; that's his specialty!"

God does not promise us that his "free" pardon costs nothing. From his side, it costs the blood of his beloved Son. On our side, it costs the consequences of our sin. We must pay for every transgression. What a man sows, that shall he reap. This is a law of life, a law of God's own ordaining, and his forgiving does not repeal or nullify that law. The promise is not that the evil we have done will be undone. The promise is that, when we receive God's forgiveness, he restores us to our place in his family, sets us on our feet again, and helps us by his grace to overcome our fault. God never says, "I have forgiven you often enough—never again! I'm through with you!"

When the great Scottish Christian and scholar George Adam Smith wrote his classic commentary on the Book of Isaiah nearly a century ago, he wrote this concerning God's promise of forgiveness, spoken by Isaiah to his sinful countrymen: "The forgiveness of God is the foundation of every bridge from a hopeless past to a courageous present." That is one of the grandest words ever spoken on this subject. Once a person knows that God has forgiven him, he is no longer at the mercy of the cruel memory and shameful consciousness of his failure. He hears God saying: "I have forgiven you that sin. Up now, stand on your feet, and walk on; henceforth rely more upon my grace and less upon your own strength and wisdom. What matters now is not how you failed in the past but that you shall succeed, prevail, overcome, in that future which begins with this moment."

The Lord enjoins us to forgive anybody against whom we

have a grievance so that our Father in heaven can forgive us our trespasses. Bertrand Russell has eloquently reminded us of how hard this can be. All around us, and in our own lives, hard cases abound; at any rate we find them hard, and some of the hardest for us might seem very trivial—to somebody else. "We pardon to the extent that we love," says La Rochefoucauld. But when we have been wronged, humiliated, hurt by another, what comes naturally to us is not love but hate. Love comes only supernaturally—in answer to our prayer; but the moment we pray for the love which we need in order to forgive, we begin to receive it, and by persevering in our prayer we shall receive it sufficiently for the hard task. It may take you twenty years, or much longer even than that, to forgive somebody from your heart; but the Lord who commands it also enables you to do it. Only, you must not quit trying until the task is done.

We have just noted that hating somebody who has wronged us seems the natural thing to do. But we always need to be careful when we think about what is "natural" in human life. It is never a self-evident and obvious matter, for what we call our ordinary human nature is warped and sick, not straight and well. In his essay "Of Revenge" Francis Bacon reminds us that "a man that studieth revenge keeps his own wounds green, which otherwise would heal and do well." Few psychological facts are better established than that. By keeping alive a grudge against our wrongdoer, we may well injure ourselves more than him. In the end, nobody suffers more from hate than the hater.

Christ restores us to our true nature, so that what seems most unnatural to our old self—loving our enemies, for example—becomes most natural to our new self in Christ: not easy, perhaps, but natural, so much so that, until we have risen to the capacity for forgiving love, we cannot enjoy that Peace which only God can give. As we forgive, so we are forgiven; as we are forgiven, we can move toward that glorious goal of our being which is conformity to Christ—the life eternal.

> Praise the Lord, O my soul, and forget not all his benefits:
>
> Who forgiveth all thy sin, and healeth all thine infirmities;
>
> Who saveth thy life from destruction, and crowneth thee with mercy and loving-kindness.
>
> Psalm 103:2–4

18

Eternal Life

The main object of religion is not to get a man into heaven but to get heaven into him.

Thomas Hardy

The Creed recalls God's creating and saving acts in the past. Then in its affirmations about the Holy Spirit, the Church, and the forgiveness of sins, it speaks of our present. Finally it speaks of our future in the resurrection of the body and the life everlasting. It is well to remind ourselves that "past," "present," and "future" are strictly human terms and categories. We cannot think meaningfully without them, and yet we know that with God there are no past, present, and future—only the Eternal Now. Our life beyond the grave will be lived in that Now, and what we now call past, present, and future will then be to us all one.

"Resurrection" is an odd word which we sometimes put to odd uses. You might say: "I went up into the attic this morning, and I resurrected an old family picture album I hadn't seen for years." It had been dead in the attic, and it came to life again as you thumbed through it. Our resurrection may be something like that to God, but only partly. The album was dead in your attic for years; you are never dead to God for a second. Through those years it was out of your mind. You are never out of God's mind. The resurrection of the album is your discovery that something you thought was dead was only sleeping. God needs no such "discovery" of you.

A resurrection-process is going on constantly in our lives. We learn as children that we get whole new bodies every seven years through the replacement of dead cells by living ones. The body dies cell by cell and is resurrected cell by cell. Likewise, our personalities, our selves, experience continuous resurrection. Personally as well as bodily you are different from yourself as you were seven years ago, or even seven minutes ago.

We are weaving our resurrection-bodies as we go along, forming our future selves in our every thought, word, and deed. What of the sins we commit? We believe in the forgiveness of sins, but, granting that, there remains this question: When we sin, even though we are forgiven, does the evil we have done get permanently incorporated into our resurrection-body? I know of no answer to that question in Scripture or in Christian doctrine. We know that a sin, being an act, has its own everlasting and irreversible consequences, as does any act, but this does not necessarily imply that it becomes an everlasting part of the sinner's own being. I think we can be sure that a sin forgiven is not a sin forgotten. Our forgiven sin is not counted against us, but we shall remember forever that, in having done the evil instead of its opposite good, we prevented the birth of some eternal blessing. And we cannot remember God's forgiveness to rejoice in his goodness and mercy except as we remember what had to be forgiven.

We can say much more certainly that whatever good we think, say, or do becomes a part of us forever, and it wonderfully helps our morale in this tough world to keep this constantly in mind. Many of the good things we want and try to do don't seem to come off, so far as we can see. But "in everything God works for good with those who love him" (Romans 8:28). We cannot see the results in our temporal now, but we shall see them in the Eternal Now and rejoice with God. Every blessed thing we try to do out of love for God and our neighbor is indeed a blessed thing, a forever abiding thing that will be through eternity a thing of beauty and a joy forever.

In the Christian vocabulary, "eternal" and "everlasting"

are not synonyms. "Everlasting" means unending. "Eternal" means Godlike, divine. He who has eternal life has God's life in him, and his life is "hid with Christ in God" (Colossians 3:3). We must learn thoroughly to think about life and death in the New Testament way. Death is not simply the cessation of animal life within the body. To hate our brother (who may be our worst enemy) is to "abide in death," and "we know that we have passed from death to life because we love the brethren" (1 John 3:13-14). To live is to love, to love is to live; to not-love is to be dead. To have eternal life is to share God's own life, which is perfect love.

Have you ever thought that it doesn't pay to be selflessly loving in this world? I was once asked to bury an old man who died friendless and alone. During his last years he had given away everything he had, even his pocket watch. People were willing enough to take and take from him, but the only ones present at his burial were his half sister, the mortician, and I. On our drive to the cemetery the half sister told me the story of his unrequited generosity and declared that such goodness doesn't pay. Of course it doesn't, in any material sense. But it "pays" in eternal life. The old gentleman knew that we pass from death to life when we love, and we may be sure that he is rejoicing and abounding in that life forever: for the eternal life which was in him is everlasting because it is in the everlasting God.

In the fifteenth chapter of First Corinthians Paul sets forth the essential Christian understanding of resurrection. He refers us to the seed planted in the ground, disappearing from our sight and apparently dying, and to the plant which springs from that seed in due season. The seed is not identical with the plant, but the nature of the seed that "died" determines the nature of the plant that springs to life. Our resurrection is something like that. The natural body in which we now live is the seed of our eternal life. This body must undergo a twofold death. It must die to self-will; as Blake puts it: "Every act of love is a little death in the divine image."

And it must undergo what we normally mean by death, the cessation of its animal functioning. When this happens it is buried in the ground, and being out of sight soon passes out of the mind and memory of our fellowmen—like that album in your attic. But God never forgets it: "Precious in the sight of the Lord is the death of his saints" (Psalm 116:15).

When he was an old man and ready to depart, John the Elder addressed his brethren: "Beloved, now are we the children of God, and it does not yet appear what we shall be; but we know that, when he shall appear, we shall be like him, for we shall see him as he is" (1 John 3:2). For many years he had lived in Christ by faith and love, starting to make heaven his home, beginning to grow in the eternal life, and now the near prospect of seeing his Lord face-to-face and entering into everlasting life with him was a joyful one. For any faithful Christian it must be so.

How are we to think about heaven and try to picture it to ourselves? Paul reminds us that "eye has not seen, nor ear heard, nor have entered into the heart of man, the things which God has prepared for those who love him" (1 Corinthians 2:9). True. Yet it would be wrong to say that we know nothing about heaven, for we know God as he shows himself to us in Christ. Heaven is that stage of life in which God's will is fully done and God's children have become altogether what God wills them to be.

In Revelation 7 we read John's report of his vision of heaven which was given to him in the Spirit. This and other Scriptures provide the material for our hope and expectation. Here are some of the truths which God has revealed to us:

Heaven is our Father's house, and in it there are rooms for all his children.

Our Lord has gone hither to prepare the right place for each of us; everything there is as he would have it.

The blessed souls in heaven are they who have come out of hard tribulation in this world and have, by God's grace, persevered to the end in their conflict with the World, the Flesh, and the Devil.

They who are before the throne of God see him face-to-face and serve him day and night. They are joyfully at home with him, and they ask no higher joy than this because it is the highest joy possible to any creature of God.

Perhaps I can best bring to a close this meditation on "the things which shall be hereafter" (Revelation 1:19) by sharing with you three words on the subject which over the years have increasingly governed my own thinking and imagining. I believe they are words of the Lord spoken to us through three true and faithful witnesses.

The first is from that strange English poet and divine, John Donne (1571?–1631), in his "Hymn to God My God, in My Sickness":

Since I am coming to that holy room,
Where, with thy choir of saints forevermore,
I shall be made thy music, as I come
I tune the instrument here at the door,
And what I must do then, think here before.

He aspires and expects to be "made God's music." Only a Christian who is also a poet would hit upon this striking metaphor. It accords with all that God reveals to us of how his continuing rule and creation of his universe makes all creation ring with "the music of the spheres." In heaven we shall not only hear that music—we shall be God's perfect instruments for the making of it.

The second of these three words was spoken by Professor A. E. Taylor (1869–1945) of Edinburgh, in *The Faith of a Moralist*. He wrote: "In the Christian heaven there is no progress, but only fruition; you are at home, and your journeys are over and done with" (vol. 1, p. 387). Later in the discussion he added: "To use the language of devout imagination, the winning of heaven would not leave the pilgrim arrived at the end of his journey with nothing further to do. In heaven itself, though there would be no longer progress *towards* fruition, there might well be progress *in* fruition. Life 'there' would be, as life 'here' is not, living by vision, as contrasted with living by faith and hope; but might not the vision itself be capable of ever-increasing enrichment?" (vol. 1, p. 408). I have learned to believe this unreservedly. Progress *toward* fruition implies, for me, a preparatory experience, an experience beginning in this life and continuing in the next. It has been variously named—Paradise, Purgatory, and the Intermediate State—by various Christians. In that experience we undergo growth toward that maturity in Christ which is readiness for heaven. When we have reached that goal, our "progress *in* fruition" can begin, and will consist in what is called, in the burial office in *The Book of Common Prayer*, going "from strength to strength, in the life of perfect service" in God's heavenly kingdom. This perfect service of God is possible only to those who have reached full fruition in the life in Christ. Such full maturation enhances all of one's powers so as to make possible such "perfect service" as is inconceivable before we reach this fruition.

Our final word is given to us by Frederick W. Robertson (1816–1853), a clergyman of the Church of England who in his young life achieved renown as a preacher. This passage is from his sermon on Eternal Life. Read it now, carefully:

"Let us think much of rest—the rest which is not of indolence but of powers in perfect equilibrium. The rest which is as deep as summer midnight, yet full of life and force as summer sunshine, the sabbath of Eternity. Let us think of the love of God, which we shall feel in its full tide upon our souls. Let us think of that marvelous career of sublime occupation which shall belong to the spirits of just men made perfect, when we shall fill a higher place in God's universe, and more consciously, and with more distinct insight, co-operate with God in the rule over his creation."

You and I have never yet experienced that rest of "powers in perfect equilibrium," but we have seen flashing foretastes of it in others and perhaps in ourselves, enough to assure and convince us that, if ever our powers are brought to such a state, we shall be able to work without wearying. The love of God even now pours at full tide upon our souls, but we do not begin to feel it as it is. In heaven we shall. Finally, "let us think of that marvelous career of sublime occupation . . . when we shall fill a higher place in God's universe, and more consciously, and with more distinct insight, co-operate with God in the rule over his creation."

That is the promise, and faithful is he who promises. If we show ourselves faithful over our few things here, he will make us masters over many things hereafter.

"And this is the record, that God has given to us eternal life, and this life is in his Son" (1 John 5:11).

"Even so, come, Lord Jesus!" (Revelation 22:20).

> O Lord, support us all the day long of this troublous life, until the shadows lengthen and the evening comes, and the busy world is hushed, and the fever of life is over, and our work is done. Then in thy mercy grant us a safe lodging, and a holy rest, and peace at the last forever.
>
> John Henry Newman